SALVAGE STYLE IN YOUR HOME

Moira and Nicholas Hankinson

SALVAGE STYLE IN YOUR HOME

Moira and Nicholas Hankinson

RODALE

RODALE

WE **INSPIRE** AND **ENABLE** PEOPLE TO IMPROVE
THEIR LIVES AND THE WORLD AROUND THEM

First published in Great Britain in 2000 by Kyle Cathie Limited,
122 Arlington Road, London NW1 7HP

Text and designs © **Moira and Nicholas Hankinson**
Photography © **Tim Winter** except those listed below.

Rodale Organic Style Books
Managing Editor: **Fern Marshall Bradley**
Project Manager: **Karen Bolesta**
Editor: **Marya Amig**
Executive Creative Director: **Christin Gangi**
Art Director: **Patricia Field**
Copy Editor: **Sarah Sacks Dunn**
Manufacturing Coordinator: **Jodi Schaffer**

Moira and Nicholas Hankinson are hereby identified as the authors of this
work.

Printed and bound in Spain by Artes Gráficas Toledo S.A.U.
D. L. TO: 1869-2000

Photo Credits
Paul Anderson: page 36; Madeleine Boulesteix: page 98 top left, page 98
right; Moira and Nicholas Hankinson: page 124 left; Bob Whitfield: page 8
center right, page 12 center right, page 37 right, page 139 bottom.

Library of Congress Cataloging-in-Publication Data
Hankinson, Moira.
    Salvage style in your home : stylish projects and inspirational ideas for
  using rescued and recycled materials to decorate your home / Moira and
  Nicholas Hankinson.
        p. cm.
  Includes bibliographical references and index.
      ISBN 0–87596–932–1 (hc)
      1. Handicraft. 2. Recycling (Waste, etc.) 3. House furnishings.
  I. Hankinson, Nicholas. II. Title.
  TT157 .H327 2000
  645—dc21
                                                                    00-011935

Distributed in the book trade by St. Martin's Press

2 4 6 8 10 9 7 5 3 1   hardcover

Contents

The decorative detail over this entrance hall arch is not carved wood, as might be expected, but an unusual hammered leather molding.

INTRODUCTION

Salvage has become newsworthy and has grown beyond the recycling of

old office buildings and factories. For many people, a sense of nostalgia is

evoked at the sight of cast-iron, claw-footed bathtubs; wooden columns;

metal window frames; weathered white marble door sills; and pile upon pile

of old clay bricks, tiles, and crates of stone, all with a history, a story to tell.

Sadly, this was not always the case. Only as recently as 30 or 40 years ago, many such items were destroyed by being put on the fire or simply thrown out. Much was gladly given away to scrap metal dealers or the junk man, who all made a living from collecting cast-offs and selling them to recyclers. If the goods had no second-hand value, huge quantities of this "waste" material were quite simply sent to the dump or local landfill.

NEAR RIGHT

Open the skillfully painted double doors of this floor-to-ceiling cupboard bought at a flea market and you will find an array of compartments filled with shelves, drawers, and hooks, as well as a fold-down table top with a perforated zinc cupboard above, which suggests it may have been used for food storage at some time.

CENTER RIGHT

An imaginative use of reclaimed materials can be seen in this exciting bathroom. Elegant Georgian stone columns flank an enormous stone bath, once housed in a psychiatric hospital, and metal scraps were cast in sea shells to make the faucet handles, while the spout was made from an old copper drainpipe. More copper piping was used to make the light above the cabinet, and the cabinet itself was constructed from old metal flashings. The slate shelf and floor edging were all found in an old schoolhouse.

FAR RIGHT

A reclaimed terrazzo floor perfectly complements an informal dining room.

Then along came a new breed of secondhand dealers that were able to see that by salvaging this debris they could make handsome profits as well as preserve our national heritage. Architectural antiques and building materials that could be reused began to find a market among designers, architects, and a few enthusiasts who frequented the newly established recycling yards and architectural salvage sales.

Further changes came about during the first of the housing booms, when the general public developed an appetite – fueled by the proliferation of new magazines and media interest – for the renovation or remodeling of neglected properties. Builders' dumpsters were raided and people stopped throwing out what had previously been considered junk. They began to realize the value of their homes, especially if they retained authentic period elements — the grander the better, reflecting wealth and status just as they always have throughout history. It was then that the demand for architectural salvage

began to grow rapidly, to such an extent that there were simply not enough supplies to satisfy the market, and specialist companies started making reproductions of architectural and period decorations.

Salvage enthusiasts have to make many decisions about their purchases. What should be done with the over-sized oak beam that looked so perfect back in the demolition yard? Should it be incorporated structurally or cosmetically? Should it be used at all? It is very easy to acquire something that then lies waiting for a home for years to come, making it more of a nuisance than a bargain.

We do not argue that because something is old it therefore merits preservation, regardless of whether it is beautiful, well designed, or even simply well made. But we do urge you to take a new look at everyday objects and question whether they, in fact, have reached the end of their useful life.

One of the goals of this book is to offer inspiration and perhaps even some answers, as well as to pass on our enormous

enthusiasm, indeed passion, for the subject of salvage. It is important ecologically to reuse materials, and we hope to stimulate thoughts and ideas of your own. This book should enlighten you on how you can create something new from something old, based on an awareness of what is available to you at a cost you can afford and using tools you already own or that are easily obtained. In this book, there are both traditional and contemporary interior photographs accompanying over 30 different projects grouped together in themed chapters: Wining and Dining; Bedrooms, Bathrooms, and Boudoirs; Rooms for Living; Decorative Accessories; Light and Shade; and Design and Detail. The projects and practical ideas are suitable for all skill levels, whether you are a beginner or a dedicated crafter.

So forget the pretentious, contrived, sterile perfection seen in so many "designer" houses, where money can purchase everything, down to the very last little detail. Free your mind from modern design ideals and lose yourself in your

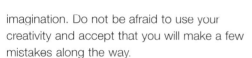

imagination. Do not be afraid to use your creativity and accept that you will make a few mistakes along the way.

Join us in our commitment to salvage and discover the pleasure in taking an object that has already had one life and turning it into something new, beautiful, and original. Through *Salvage Style in Your Home* we try to communicate our ideas and explore the almost limitless possibilities for creatively reusing, reinventing, revitalizing, and reinterpreting good-quality materials.

RIGHT

Everything in the bathroom of this converted mid-nineteenth century church has been salvaged. Curved paneling taken from the canopy above the organ has been cleverly used to disguise pipes, the cistern has been hidden behind a pew, and the window sill finished off with a slate shelf.

A large table automatically becomes the focal point in a dining area because it is the place not only for eating and drinking but also a place where family and friends spend time top is wooden, the beauty of the grain and the warmth of the wood may contrast with the surroundings of many of today's minimal, cool interiors. It may be a simple, functional design, with

WINING AND DINING

together, gathering for discussions, celebrations, and even business meetings. When you sit down at a table you immediately see and make contact with the table top, whether it is wood (the material traditionally used to build tables), zinc, stainless steel, stone, or slate, all of which are good materials for rejuvenating an old table, depending on the surrounding decor. If the table a scrubbed plank top; an oak, ash, or elm surface supported on a trestle base; or it may be something on a larger scale, even grander, perhaps made from hardwood with a highly polished surface and elegantly tapered legs. Whatever the style, a table may appear easy to design and make, but getting the design and proportions absolutely right can be quite a challenge.

NEAR RIGHT

Pine dressers rarely have such visual impact. The top half of this dresser, displaying white china that is used daily, was made with reclaimed wood and then painted to match the old original base.

CENTER LEFT

This circular kitchen table top was salvaged, repainted, and screwed to a cast-iron base made from an agricultural stump grinder (still bearing the manufacturer's name) to make a unique yet practical piece of furniture.

CENTER RIGHT

Slate slabs from a country farmhouse floor were made into tables, and the wheels from an old railroad cart were used to make the bases. The decorative bracket was once a tavern sign, and the window glass, coping stones, and wooden floor were all recycled.

FAR RIGHT

An ornate gilded theater box was located, refurbished, and installed to great dramatic effect above the double folding doors leading from this elegant hotel dining room.

LEFT

Despite its contemporary look, much of this kitchen has been salvaged. Both the zinc sheets on the walls and the faucets on the left side of the counter came from an old hospital, while the column and twin radiators were bought from a recycling yard. The door handles in the background are old trap door pull rings, and the curving kitchen counter came from a barroom at an old country inn.

A wooden table top needs protection from very hot dishes, which can damage its surface. Practical, good-looking table mats are often difficult to find, but slate roofing tiles are readily available either from someone who is reroofing his home or from salvage yards found across the country. Cut down to size, varnished, and backed with felt, the slate tiles make stunning, indispensable place mats. (By mixing wedges of tongue-and-groove wood paneling scraps in different colors and joining them together, you can make another unusual place mat.) To finish dressing the table, use old aluminum dishes, which have been given an authentic pewter look and put to use as chargers, coordinating beautifully with the slate mats. Use clean, empty tins filled with flowers and foliage, and give new life to old bedsprings as quirky candle holders (see page 122). To complete the look, recycle curtains, cushion covers, sheets, tablecloths, or any other suitable fabric from garage sales and thrift shops into napkins.

Traditionally, dining chairs were made from oak, elm, ash, fruitwood, or a combination of these woods in hundreds of different designs. Many of these designs are still reproduced today, though most are crafted in beech or pine.

Robust benches often make a convenient alternative to chairs where space is limited in an informal dining area, and they can be made quite easily using old scaffold boards. We show how a simple three-legged stool can be put together using a wooden chopping board for the seat and ash axe handles for the legs, just as salvaged tractor seats can be made into comfortable kitchen stools.

With the warmth of the fire and the glow of the lights, wining and dining is surely one of life's great pleasures.

SLATE TABLE MATS

EQUIPMENT

Tape measure
Straight edge
Marking point or sharp nail
Slate ripper
Pliers
Electric sander (optional)
Medium-grit sandpaper
½-inch paintbrush
Scissors
Glue brush

MATERIALS

Eight roof slates, overall size approx.
   6 x 12 inches
Four larger roof slates, overall size approx.
   20 x 14 inches
Satin finish or floor-grade varnish
Approx. 2½ square yards felt
Rubberized glue

The materials above are sufficient to make a set of eight table mats and four center mats. Adjust measurements as necessary according to the size of roof slates available. Also bear in mind the size of the table on which they will be placed.

METHOD

1 Select your slates carefully, rejecting any that are splitting, are too irregular in shape, or have enlarged nail holes. Measure the slates from a good end and score a line across each width with the marking point or sharp nail. Use the slate ripper to cut the slates to size, being careful to keep the cut edge as straight as possible. We suggest that the 16-x-12-inch slates are cut down to 12 x 8 inches and the 20-x-14-inch slates are cut down to 14 x 11 inches.

2 All hand-split and cut slates have one face that is usually flat, while the other has a chipped beveled edge. The face with the beveled edge will be the top of your place mat. Use pliers to trim the cut edge and the original edges to remove any loose material, matching the original beveled edges if possible. Remove any loose material from both faces and finish with sandpaper, either by hand or by using the electric sander, taking care not to score the top surface too heavily. Wash each slate carefully in running water and let it dry.

3 When both surfaces are dry, paint them with two coats of satin finish or floor-grade varnish, covering any indentations and the beveled edges. Let them dry.

4 Cut 12 pieces of felt ½ inch smaller around than the size of the slates. Brush rubberized glue on the underside of the slates and fit the felt onto the bottom surface; this will prevent your table mats from scratching the table surface.

Safety note

Wear safety glasses or goggles when using any mechanical sanding equipment. Rubber or protective gloves are also recommended for this project.

Food is one of our growing passions – if the number of cookbooks and television programs is any indication – and the social importance of family meals is widely recognized. Yet how much thought do we give to the presentation of the daily eating ritual? Making the table look as exciting as the dishes themselves takes just a little thought and effort, and here's one way to rejuvenate roof slates to make easy but chic replacements for melamine mats bearing images of Niagara Falls and Mount Rushmore. These slate mats will give your table a new, crisp image, and by scouring dumpsters parked outside properties in the process of being reroofed, demolished, or restored, you are sure to find enough slates to make up a table setting for 10 or more. (Always seek the contractor's or homeowner's permission before removing anything from a construction dumpster.)

If "dumpster diving" is not your style, another source of old roofing slate is your nearest reclamation yard. The slate will have been exposed to wind, rain, snow, and pollution, but it will still be desirable. Newly cut slate can be purchased from any flooring contractor, tile shop, or roofing supplier, where you will be faced with a mind-boggling selection of color, size, and thickness.

Damaged or chipped roofing slates can be cut down to the required size and the underside covered in felt to protect the table surface. Once cleaned and polished, the slate's inherent insulating qualities, combined with its practical wipe-clean surface, make it a smart table accessory.

INFORMAL DINING

There is a proliferation of companies selling sunrooms and greenhouses whose pitch has long been to persuade us to take the "inside out," but the owners of this country kitchen decided to bring the "outside in" when it came to decorating an informal family eating area.

Inspired by their potting shed and a collection of old tools – most of which were handmade, although some of their origins were rather obscure – the homeowners' interpretation of this informal look began to take shape with the tool display, not the table, being the focal point. Although the potting shed was fairly old, its interior had been insensitively modernized at some stage in its history, leaving little of its original charm. With a blank canvas and a limited budget, the owners set to work.

Natural light was poor, so the walls were painted off-white and an old exterior barn door, complete with its original chipped and flaking paint, was installed. In order to make the shed more intimate, they disguised the ceiling with suspended rows of old wooden ladders. This gave the room a warmer, more welcoming feel and provided a place to hang baskets, herbs, and other decorative items. The ladders were obtained very inexpensively from a quaint, old-fashioned horticultural nursery that closed its doors after the death of its elderly owner. The ladders, which were considered unsafe once they were superseded by their modern metal counterparts, had not been used for some time.

The classic monastery table was made from recycled scaffold boards, and the chapel chairs came from an old church, as their name suggests. A stool was made using axe handles in ash for the legs. Soft, atmospheric lighting in the form of a floor-standing candle lamp was created from a flower display stand, and a stencil candle light was added to make an interesting table centerpiece. To complete the look, assorted garden sieves and an old saw were hung as attractive wall displays, and faux pewter plates were used to adorn the windowsill.

TOOL DISPLAY

Old farm equipment, kitchen utensils, and garden tools are still easy to find, inexpensive to buy, and have a character sadly missing in many of the implements produced today.

Avid readers of local newspapers will find auctions and garage or yard sales advertised extensively. As small growers and farmers retire, their families are reluctant to continue to work on what are often unprofitable holdings, and the land is sold to surrounding farmers or is purchased by urban dwellers seeking a rural retreat. This leads to the sale of the everyday tools used by past generations. Many of the tools were made by local foundries or were fabricated by the landowner using skills now forgotten.

Walls displaying old shovels, pitchforks, and rakes of odd shapes and sizes, some complete, a few broken, and many of a uniquely local design, are a constant source of intrigue. For this project, we have used a selection of farm and garden tools displayed on an old wooden door. The tools include an old spring grain scale with a brass face that was only revealed after layers of dirt were scrubbed off, a hand-forged drainage spade, a pruning saw, a short flat-tined fork (the origin of which remains unknown), a brass and iron stirrup pump, a primitive sickle, and a pair of fencing pliers. These tools were only a small part of a selection of grimy and broken tools bought as one lot at a farm auction for less than half the price of a modern hand trowel.

EQUIPMENT

1-inch paintbrush
Waxing brush or stiff-bristled paintbrush
Soft cotton rags
Fine-grade steel wool
Metal polish
Wire brush
Electric drill
Circular wire brush or sanding wheel
⅛-inch wood drill bit
Screwdriver
Pliers

MATERIALS

Selection of old tools
Wooden braced plank display board
Colorless wood preservative
Antique brown furniture wax
Clear wax or clear lacquer spray
Selection of screws and rawlplugs
Medium metal wire or gardening wire
Length of wood approx. 1 x 3 inches x the
    width of the display board

Safety note

Wear safety glasses or goggles when using any mechanical sanding equipment. Rubber or other protective gloves are recommended for this project.

TOOL DISPLAY

METHOD

1 Treat the display board with colorless wood preservative and let it dry. Then apply antique brown furniture wax with the waxing brush or stiff-bristled paintbrush. Rub the wax into the wood with a soft cotton rag and polish it to a soft sheen with another rag. Apply a second coat of wax to give the board a deeper color and longer-lasting finish. Set the board aside.

2 To clean brass or copper surfaces, use metal polish and fine-grade steel wool, finishing with more polish applied with a soft cotton rag. Seal the polished surfaces with the clear lacquer spray to prevent tarnishing. Wash wooden handles and parts in warm soapy water and then wax and polish them with the furniture wax. Clean iron or steel tools with a wire brush to remove loose rust and dirt, then finish them with the electric drill fitted with the circular wire brush or a sanding wheel.

3 Use the drill and circular wire brush or sanding wheel to remove corrosion until the desired finish is achieved. The metal surface of the tool will be pitted more or less deeply depending on the amount of corrosion it has suffered; the goal of this cleaning is not to return the tool to its original condition but to remove surface rust and reveal the color of the base metal. To preserve the finish and prevent corrosion, either apply clear wax to the surface of the tool or spray it with clear lacquer.

4 Place the display board on two blocks above a flat surface so that you can work from both sides, and experiment with arranging the cleaned tools on the front until you have a display that pleases you. Wooden-handled tools can be attached to the board using screws driven in from the back of the display board. Remove each tool, carefully noting its position, and use the electric drill and ⅛-inch drill bit to drill a hole from the front of the display board into the area where the handle will be placed. Replace the tool and, working from the back of the board, drive a screw through the board and into the handle, securing the tool to the board.

5 Metal tools can be fitted to the board using the medium metal wire or garden wire. Use a malleable coated wire of a muted color or one with a dull finish, otherwise the wire will be obvious and spoil the appearance of the finished display. Select a part of the tool that will support it when the board is returned to its upright position and drill holes close to each side of the tool. Cut a length of wire, bend it into a "U" shape, then pass it over the tool and through both holes so that each end emerges by at least 2 inches on the back of the display board. Use pliers to twist the ends of wire together to secure the tool to the board.

When all the tools are attached, remove the board from the blocks and place it upright to ensure that all the tools are securely in place. Tighten any screws or wire or add more if needed. Take the 1-x-3-inch wooden board and attach it to the wall using the screws and rawlplugs. Place the display board on the wall, resting a brace on the 1-x-3-inch board. Once you are satisfied with the position of the display board, secure it with two screws through the board into the 1-x-3-inch board.

FLOWER DISPLAY CANDLE STAND

EQUIPMENT

Wire brush
Small stiff brush (an old toothbrush
    is ideal)
½-inch paintbrush
Soft brush or cotton rags

MATERIALS

Flower stand
Stove blacking paste
Selection of small metal tart and
    confectionery cups
Matte black paint or spray paint
Tea lights
Candle
Scented oils

Safety note

Rubber or protective gloves are
recommended for this project.

Auctions are good hunting grounds for interesting items. We bought several "bargains" at the auction of the contents of a nursery and garden center, including a number of cast-iron stands once used to display bunches of fresh-cut flowers.

The stands had not been used for many years, and the original paint had almost completely rusted away. Constructed of a hollow iron column set in a heavy cast hexagonal base, each stand came with a number of bent metal display platforms designed to fit over the column and be fixed at any height using a turn-screw. As expected, there was little demand at the auction for these peculiar items, and we were able to buy them for next to nothing. It is unlikely that similar stands are easy to find, but the new use we found for them illustrates how, by using a little imagination, the most unwanted items can be salvaged and revived. Place plain or fluted individual metal confectionery tins (individual aluminum pie tins will work just as well) into the metal platforms and fill some with tea lights and others with aromatic essential oils – to please the eye and soothe the senses. Alternatively, remove the platforms, keeping just the heavy bases and pole, and have an electrician wire the stand — unless you are confident enough to undertake this yourself — and convert it into a lamp. Painted and fitted with a simple shade, the display stand takes on a cool contemporary look, far removed from its original purpose.

FLOWER DISPLAY CANDLE STAND

METHOD

1 We gave our candelabra a muted satin black finish. (Had the stand been completely rusted rather than patchy with some of the original paint still attached, we would have wire-brushed it and sealed the finish with a clear lacquer to preserve its appearance.) Remove the metal platforms (each comprised of two sets of four branches welded to a central pipe) from the column and make sure the turn-screws work freely; apply lubricating oil if necessary. Use the wire brush to remove loose rust and peeling paint from the base, column, and platforms, making sure to wire-brush any residual paint to prepare the surface for the stove blacking finish.

2 Place the stand and platforms on newspaper or another protective surface and, with the small stiff brush, apply the stove blacking to all of the exposed parts, paying particular attention to the corroded metal and making sure that all the surfaces are covered. Let the stand and platforms dry to a matte black finish. When the blacking is completely dry, polish the stand and platforms to a soft sheen with a soft brush or cotton rag. Continue polishing until the rag picks up little or no polish and the blacking does not come off when the stand is handled. Replace the platforms on the stand in the positions desired, and secure with the turn-screws.

3 For the candle holders, we used a selection of round and fluted metal tart and confectionery cups. Old, rusty, and long past their useful life, the cups were found in a local thrift store, and they fit the platform rings perfectly. Brush or spray paint the cups matte black, both inside and out, and let them dry. Place a tea light into each cup and fit the cups into the rings. We inserted tea lights into the larger cups and filled the smaller fluted cups with scented oils. Finally, fit a candle into the top of the stand. Light the candle and the tea lights. As the candles warm the oils in the fluted cups, the oils' perfume will permeate the room.

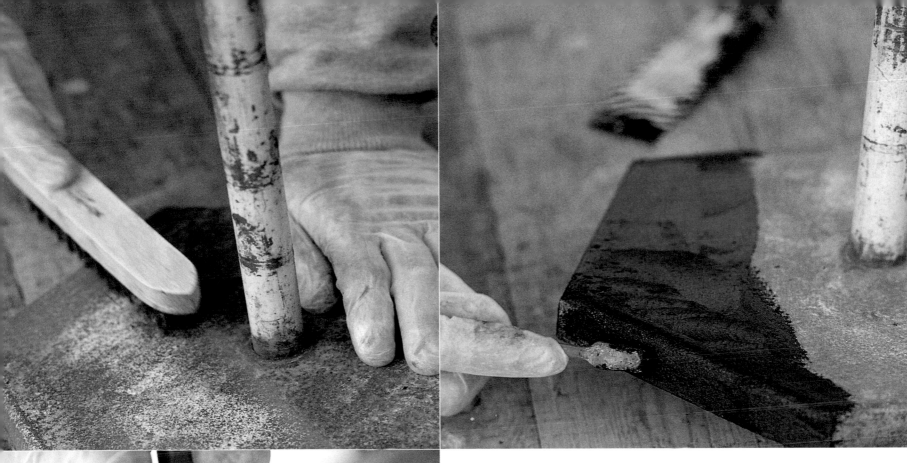

STENCIL LIGHT

EQUIPMENT

Scissors or craft knife

MATERIALS

18 equally sized metal stencils, either
    letters or numbers
Aluminum foil adhesive tape
Candle and candle holder

METHOD

1 Select half of the stencils and place them front side down on a flat surface. Carefully arrange them together to make a rectangle three stencils wide by three stencils deep. Most old stencils were hand cut, so their sizes will be slightly irregular. When fitting them together, make sure that the edges of your rectangle are square.

2 Use the scissors or craft knife to cut lengths of the aluminum foil adhesive tape to the height and width of the rectangle. Carefully remove the tape backing and lay the tape along the joints between the stencils to join them together, using a finger to rub down the tape to secure it in place. Repeat with the remaining nine stencils to make a second, similarly sized rectangle.

3 Cut two lengths of tape to the height of the rectangles. Remove the backing from one piece of tape and join the two rectangles to make one piece six stencils wide by three deep. Carefully bring the two ends of the rectangle together to make a cylinder; place your hand inside and join the ends together with the remaining cut length of tape. Again, rub down all newly taped joints with your finger to make sure they are secure.

Stand the candle holder and candle on a flat surface and place the newly constructed stencil light over them. The metal tape should be sufficiently malleable to allow the stencils to be manipulated into a hexagonal shape. Light the candle and enjoy the muted illumination cast from this simple, yet charming candle light.

Stencils have been used for many years to mark cartons, boxes, crates, bales, and all sorts of goods. Made from a variety of materials including zinc, steel, tin, cardboard, and even brass, stencils are still in use today, although most modern stencil designs are manufactured from molded plastic. We have managed to amass several full sets of metal stencils over the years; most are made of zinc but one particularly valued set is made from copper sheet. For this project, we have used a set of more commonly available zinc stencils that came from a farm auction and were bought in their original box complete with brushes and inks. The stencils had been heavily used and were stained with ink, but we chose to use them in this condition rather than attempt to clean them.

The joy of stencils, when used for a lighting project such as this, is that the lettering cut-outs cast curious illuminations, creating a charming display of light and shade. This project is a very basic candle light, but the more experienced craftsperson might attempt the construction of a light column, shade, or wall light.

PEWTER PLATES

EQUIPMENT

Metal cleaning paste
Medium-grade steel wool
Soft cotton rags

MATERIALS

Aluminum plates or bowls
Metal polish
Antique brown furniture wax
Clear lacquer spray

METHOD

1 Carefully select the plates or bowls you will be using for this project. They will show the effects of years of wear and tear and will be scored with cutlery marks very similar to the surface markings seen on most antique pewter, but this is part of their charm. Do not use plates that are stamped with a manufacturer's mark on their top surface. Instead, choose plates that are unmarked and are not too damaged or dented.

2 Place a small amount of metal cleaner (we used a stainless steel cleaner) on an old plate or other container, dip a wad of steel wool in the cleaner, and begin to work on the surface of the plate. Always rub around the surface and keep the wad of steel wool saturated with cleaner. Continue working until any surface oxidation is removed and the steel wool is worked into the surface of the aluminum. Periodically wipe the surface clean with a soft cotton rag to examine the finish. Be careful not to rub out all the surface scratches and markings.

3 When you are satisfied with the appearance of the plate, wipe it clean and apply the metal polish with a soft cotton rag, rubbing it well into the surface. Wipe the surface clean and polish it with another clean soft cloth. Now examine the plate and decide on its final color and finish. The cleaner and polish will have darkened the appearance of the plate, but an even darker finish can be achieved by rubbing a little antique brown furniture wax into the surface. Apply the wax liberally and wipe it off, leaving a residue on the surface. Let it dry and then polish it. You may want to stop at this point because the wax will prevent further tarnishing.

4 If you want a glossy finish, spray the plate with clear lacquer and let it dry. Your faux pewter plates will deceive all but the most perceptive observers, unless they pick them up, in which case their light weight will reveal the fraud. Display the plates on a dresser or shelf, hang them on a wall, or use them as chargers under plates on the dining room table. Lacquered plates can be washed in hot water, and waxed plates should be dusted clean. None of the plates should be used for eating purposes.

Safety note

Wear rubber or protective gloves for this project and work on newspaper or some other disposable surface.

Pewter is an alloy of tin and lead, and sometimes a little copper or antimony. In the past, pewter was used for plates, mugs, and other vessels as a substitute for wooden or porous earthenware vessels. Lead is highly toxic, so do not use early pewter for food or drink. Because of this danger, modern pewter is made with considerably less lead.

Early pewter is very collectable and fetches high prices at auctions or in antique shops. When polished, it has a dull, attractive sheen, and a collection of old pewter arranged on a dresser or mantle makes a memorable display.

Recently we discovered a number of discarded aluminum plates and bowls that we thought might lend themselves to conversion into faux pewter. This project demonstrates our method.

AXE-HANDLE STOOL

EQUIPMENT

Tape measure
Electric drill
1-inch spade wood bit
½-inch straight or rounded wood chisel
Hammer or mallet
Variable-speed multipurpose electric tool
 with ¾-inch sanding head (or round
 wood file)
Soft cotton rags
Medium-grit sandpaper

MATERIALS

Round piece of wood approx. 14 inches
 diameter x 1½ inches thick
Three axe handles or three 24-inch lengths
 of broom handle
Wood scraps
Wood glue

Many of the "bargains" found in a reclamation yard or scavenged from a construction dumpster remain in our workshop to this day, half forgotten, awaiting the visionary ideas for which they were originally acquired.

One such purchase was a stack of dirt-encrusted axe handles found at a country auction. Their interesting shapes caught our eye, and on closer inspection we realized they were made of solid ash. We managed to purchase some, and now we wish we had bought more.

The shape of the axe handles seemed to suggest legs, and so we used three of them for the legs of a kitchen chopping block. In this project, we show how they can also be used to construct a charming if unconventional stool. A discarded round piece of beech wood, probably originally made as a chopping board, was used to make the seat.

The axe handles also could be used to make the sides of a log basket, and, if you could buy a large number of them, they would make an eye-catching balustrade. If you can't find axe handles, the stool can be made just as easily from broom handles or straight branches pruned from a tree.

When making this stool, the legs should be slightly splayed for stability, and all the holes that hold the legs should be cut at a slight angle to allow for the splay. For the seat of the stool, a similar round piece can be cut from a solid or laminated wood scrap.

AXE-HANDLE STOOL

METHOD

1 Mark three points on the top surface at an equal distance around the circumference of the round piece of wood and approximately 1 inch from the edge. Place the axe handles or other material being used for the legs inside these marked points and trace around them with a pencil to mark where the legs will be inserted into the seat of the stool.

2 Place the round piece of wood (the seat) on a piece of scrap wood and use the spade bit, driven in at a slight angle, to make an initial hole. To prevent the wood from splitting, drill from one side of the seat until the point of the spade bit just emerges, and then finish drilling the hole from the opposite side. Repeat, drilling holes for all three legs. If you are using broom handles for the legs, use a spade bit the size of the handles.

3 Use the variable-speed multipurpose electric sander or chisel and wood file to enlarge the holes to the size of the pencil marks, making sure that the angles of the splays are maintained. If you are making the legs from broom handles, you should not have to enlarge the spade-drilled holes.

4 Apply wood glue liberally to the first 1 inch of each of the axe handles and insert them into the holes in the seat from the underside. Tap them gently with a hammer or mallet until the tops are flush with the upper surface of the seat. Axe handles are made with a slit cut into their top to allow a wedge to be inserted when fitted to the axe head. Cut a small wedge from scrap wood the width of this slit, apply glue, and drive it into the top of the handle to secure it firmly into the seat of the stool. If you are using broom handle pieces for legs, cut a 1½-inch slit in the top of each piece to so you can wedge them into the seat for added security and strength.

Wipe off any excess glue and set the stool on one side until the glue dries. Sand off any excess glue or wood from the top surface and finish as desired. The stool can be waxed, stained, or painted. If you stain it, make sure that any glue on the wood surface is removed before you apply the stain because the dried glue will not absorb the stain and then the finish will be patchy. The stool top we made for this project was completed with a distressed paint finish, and the legs were waxed with antique brown furniture wax.

An oak bed made from 200-year-old beams taken from the roof of a barn that had collapsed as a result of neglect. The headboard insert is natural woven willow.

Whether the style is comfortably traditional or has a Zen-like simplicity, bedrooms are where we spend a third of our lives. Careful thought and consideration need to be given

The amount of light in a bedroom largely depends on the direction in which the room faces, and light, whether daylight or interior lighting, helps to dictate a bedroom's mood and colors.

BEDROOMS, BATHROOMS, AND BOUDOIRS

to how we treat our bedrooms, which are certainly the most personal rooms in the house, if not the most important. Besides the bed, a bedroom may have space for additional furniture, perhaps an armchair, sofa, or table, as well as storage items such as chests of drawers and wardrobes. Bedrooms are not only a place to sleep but also a place to spend time reading and relaxing.

Antique decorating fabrics are fun to use for bedcovers, cushions, loose covers, and throws for the chairs. For years, linen has been a favorite — especially old, high-quality linen sheets, roughly textured, often with a red embroidered monogram and occasionally a fringed edge. They make simple but beautiful draping curtains, allowing light to filter softly into the bedroom.

Children have their own ideas when it comes to decorating their bedrooms, and strong, bright colors usually appeal to them. They like their own special piece of furniture, such as an old school desk that has been rescued and transformed from a grubby object covered with graffiti into something revitalized, practical, and fun. Older children and teenagers use their bedrooms to escape from parents and grown-ups. There, surrounded by a chaotic mess, they can play loud music, hence the need for CD storage. In this chapter, we show you how to make practical CD storage out of a dilapidated old wooden shutter (see pages 54–57).

The bed is an obvious feature or focal point in the bedroom. Beds are made from many different materials, most commonly wood, iron, or brass. However, a bed made from an unusual material such as aluminum will give a very contemporary feel to a bedroom. Beds come in all shapes and sizes. Although there are manufacturers that will make up mattresses in unusual dimensions, including round or even boat-shaped, bear in mind when constructing a bed from your own design that mattresses are easier and cheaper to obtain in standard sizes. Whatever its size and shape, your mattress should be the best quality you can afford.

Finding wood that is suitable for building beds is often easier than you think. Old railway sleepers and ceiling beams of oak and elm can all be cut to size to make the framework, while carved doors, church pews, decorative wooden panels, and even farm gates are the perfect raw materials for making practical and interesting headboards. A highly unusual fold-away guest bed is shown on the opposite page. It was imaginatively made from an exquisitely painted panel depicting animals from Noah's Ark that was salvaged from a fairgrounds amusement ride.

The idea that bathrooms should be spartan, purely functional, hygienic rooms containing a cast-iron bathtub, pedestal sink, toilet, and linoleum-covered floor is fortunately long gone.

Bathrooms today are expected to be every bit as comfortable as any other room in the house. Just take a look through any of the glossy magazines available today, and you will see rooms purporting to be bathrooms but looking more like stage sets – all opulence and atmosphere – or the epitome of rustic country charm – cozy and homely. Unusual items add interest and character, such as a single scaffold bracketed to the wall and used as a rail to show off pretty towels and linens (see pages 42–43). Enormous cupboards in rich mahogany or other hardwoods, too big and cumbersome for the average-sized room today, can be cut down in size to panel a bath or perhaps used to create cupboards under the sink, providing additional storage.

Because we lead increasingly busy lives with more and more pressures, there seems to be a need to simplify things, to have order, comfort, and harmony in our homes. One way of achieving this is to optimize space and create additional storage areas – a place for everything and everything in its place. Old hardwood rail compartments can be salvaged and made into spacious cupboards for the dressing room or boudoir. Enormous, superbly carved mahogany wardrobes, which would be extremely expensive if the equivalent quality were made today, look just as handsome and majestic when made to fit a small alcove.

TOP LEFT

This unusual spare bed, which folds up against the wall when not in use, is an original 1933 Noah's Ark amusement ride, comprising two horses and chariots. On the bed is a salvaged queen-sized bedcover, and in the background is a mural painted to disguise a wall-to-wall cupboard containing an office desk and storage.

TOP RIGHT

Black and white are used with striking effect in this guest bathroom, its 1930s fixtures juxtaposed with contemporary lighting.

RIGHT

The shower walls and mirror frame in this bathroom were made from old sheet-metal roofing, and the soap dich/shampoo rack were created from a lightning conductor salvaged from a church. The sink was cleverly fashioned from the base of an old copper hot water tank, and the faucet handles were cast from metal roof flashing in a gelatin mold.

RAILWAY BED

EQUIPMENT

Tape measure
Steel square
Hammer
1¼-inch wood chisel
Handsaw
Sandpaper
Electric drill and bits
Screwdriver
Adjustable wrench
1-inch paintbrush
Soft cotton rags

MATERIALS

Four wooden posts
Approx. 6 feet 6 inches of 9-x-1-inch
    planed wood
Wood glue
2½-inch wood screws
Single metal bed frame and
    headboard fittings
Wood stain
Clear furniture wax

Amid the pile of debris, our eyes were drawn to the tapered wooden poles protruding above the rusty metal boxes, bed frames stacked one upon the other, and assorted shovels.

Filthy, wet, and shivering, we stood in the biting wind on a November morning speculating on what the poles had been used for and how they could be used again. Inspiration struck! Their slender shapes lent themselves perfectly to a design for a bed – a four-poster bed to be precise. We later learned from the owner of the salvage yard that the poles were solid ash levers used on the railroads to move wagons around the sidings by hand before mechanization made them obsolete. If you can't get ash levers such as these, the bed could just as easily be constructed using any pillar-like objects, such as fence posts or staircase newel posts.

The metal bed frame and headboard fittings were located in a scrap yard. Almost 40 years old, they had once been turned out by the thousands. They were manufactured for use in army barracks but had never been used. Apart from some surface rust, they were in perfect condition. If you can't find a similar frame, you can buy one new from a furniture maker. This bed could also be made with a slatted wooden base set into wooden side pieces fitted to the headboard using any of the numerous connectors on the market.

RAILWAY BED

METHOD

Before starting this project, read all of the instructions and think carefully about the dimensions of your bed and how you will make it. Remember that you will need to find or purchase a mattress for the bed and that most are made to standard sizes. As a guide, single beds are normally constructed so that the mattress top is approximately 18 to 20 inches from the floor, and you will have to adapt the project to the mattress you will use. If you want to provide storage under the bed, the frame can be made higher, although it is a good idea to keep it to a height at which you can sit comfortably on the edge of the bed.

1 Make a mark with a pencil at the proposed height of the bed frame on the inside face of one of the posts. Place the headboard fitting on the post so that the bed frame will be attached at that height. Mark the screw holes and make two marks, one above and one below each screw hole, 4 inches apart, centered on the screw hole. Use the steel square to transfer these measurements across the inside and down two sides of the post. Measure the exact thickness of the 9-inch wooden plank and draw a line that measurement deep on the two sides across the 4-inch pencil lines. Use the hammer and wood chisel to score a line along this mark, which shows the areas to be cut out of the post to house the 9-inch head- and footboards. Turn the inside of the post face up and with a handsaw make a series of cuts approximately ½ inch apart and 1 inch deep, using the chiseled line as a guide for the exact depth, for the full length of the 4-inch marked area.

2 After you have made saw cuts across the whole width of the post, insert the wood chisel into the cuts and gently pry out the waste wood. Clean the cut mortise with the wood chisel and sandpaper, making sure to keep to the depth indicated by the scored lines. Now repeat this process using another post. These two posts will hold the headboard.

3 Measure the exact width of your bed frame from fixing bolt (or bolt hole) to fixing bolt. Measure the width of a post and add it to this measurement. Use the steel square to mark that final measurement on the planed wooden plank and cut it to size. Lay the cut plank on a work surface and use the steel square and pencil to mark a line the width of the post across each end. Mark two lines 4 inches apart at each end centered on the width of the plank, and extend them to join the lines marking the width of the post. Use the handsaw to cut away the two outer sections at each end, each of which will measure approximately 2½ inches by the width of the post, to create a simple tenon at each end. Be careful when cutting; it is better to cut off too little wood and to have to sand down the joints to fit the mortises cut in the posts, than to remove too much wood and be left with loose joints.

4 Put plenty of wood glue into the mortise in the first post, then insert one of the tenons. Use the steel square to check that the joint is true, then drill and secure with 2½-inch wood screws. Before finally joining the pieces, replace the headboard fitting and check that its screw holes do not correspond with the screws holding the joint. Repeat this process with the second post, and you have created the headboard for your bed. Wipe off any excess wood glue and set the assembled pieces aside until the glue

dries completely. Now follow steps 3 and 4 to construct the footboard with the second two posts and remaining wooden plank.

5 Replace the headboard fittings on the footboard and headboard, and secure them with screws driven through the joints into the wooden posts.

6 You will probably need help with this part of the project. Lean the headboard against a vertical surface and balance one end of the bed frame on its headboard fittings. Raise the other end of the frame and maneuver the footboard so that the bed frame can be dropped into place over its fittings. Half-tighten the integral nuts on the bed frame to secure it first to the footboard then to the headboard. Use a wrench to tighten all the nuts to make a rigid frame.

When we assembled the bed, we decided that because the colors of the ash wood bed posts and the salvaged pitch pine end boards were so different, we would stain the whole bed a uniform medium oak color. This also masked the lighter tones of the exposed wood where the ends had been sawed. After applying the stain with a cotton rag, we finished the bed with a light coat of clear furniture wax and polished it with another soft cotton rag. Installed in a spare room and fitted with a mattress, the bed was made up with a cotton-covered duvet and down-filled pillow along with a natural sheepskin thrown over its foot.

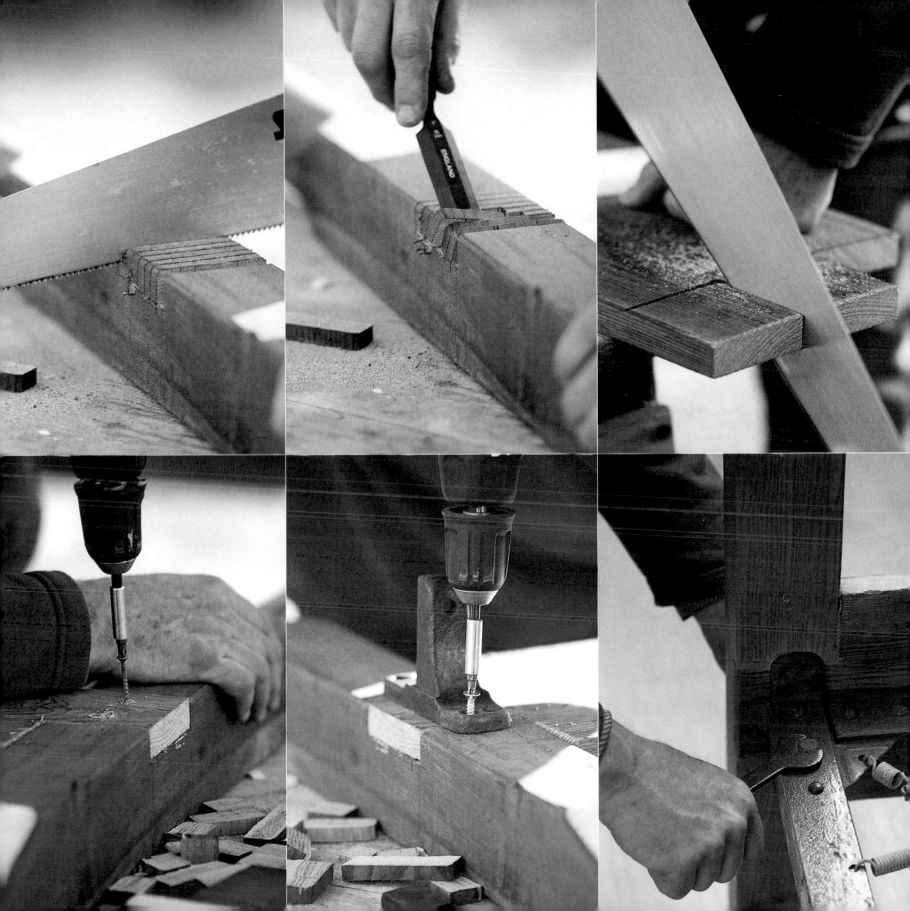

SCAFFOLD TOWEL RAIL

EQUIPMENT

Tape measure
Handsaw
Paint scraper
Electric sander
Sandpaper
1¾-inch paintbrush
Soft cotton rags
Electric hammer drill
Masonry drill bit
Wood drill bit to fit 2½-inch screws
Screwdriver

MATERIALS

Wooden scaffold
White translucent wood finish or white
    matte acrylic paint and satin finish
    acrylic varnish
2-x-3-inch spruce or pine stud
2½-inch rawlpugs
2½-inch screws
Four 1½-inch angle (or corner) brackets
¾-inch screws

Safety note

Wear safety glasses or goggles
when using any mechanical
sanding equipment; a dust mask
also should be worn in case the
surface to be sanded was
previously finished with a lead-
based paint. Rubber or protective
gloves are also recommended for
this project.

METHOD

1 Measure the site where the towel rail will be installed, then measure the scaffold. If the scaffold is too long to fit in the selected site, allowing for at least a 6-inch gap below the scaffold and a similar or larger gap above, trim it to size with the handsaw. Remove flaked or loose paint with the paint scraper, and sand the scaffold to a smooth finish with the electric sander and sandpaper. It is not necessary to remove all residual paint, just enough to produce a smooth base for the wood finish. Use the electric sander to smooth off any sharp edges or corners.

2 Apply a liberal coat of white translucent wood finish or matte white acrylic paint. Wait a few minutes until the finish or paint is partially dry, then wipe over the surface with a clean cotton rag to remove some of the surface color, leaving a residual finish on the wood surface. Repeat this process until you get your desired result. Let the scaffold dry. If you have used matte acrylic paint, seal the scaffold with two coats of satin finish acrylic varnish.

3 Measure the width of the scaffold at the top and bottom rungs, then use the handsaw to cut two lengths of the 2-x-3-inch spruce or pine stud to these measurements to make wall supports. Ideally, these should be painted in the same color as the wall on which the scaffold towel rail is to be fitted; if not, they should be finished to match the scaffold. Add 6 inches to the height of the scaffold, and use the drill and masonry drill bit to attach the top support to the wall at this point with rawlplugs and 2½-inch screws. Place the scaffold against the wall, mark the position of the bottom rung on the wall, and then attach the bottom support in the same way. This will raise the scaffold base approximately 6 inches off the floor. Fit the 1½-inch angle (or corner) brackets on the back of the scaffold behind the top and bottom rungs with the ¾-inch screws, positioning them so that when the scaffold is mounted on the supports, the brackets will be concealed behind the rungs of the scaffold. Secure the scaffold to the supports with more ¾-inch screws.

Flipping through the pages of today's magazines you will see bamboo and wooden ladders used as props in interior photographs because they make wonderful display stands. Our towel rack is not a ladder but a scaffold, often used in the painting and decorating trades as a portable wooden platform. The scaffold had been painted at some point, and rather than sand the paint off, we chose to keep its worn and aged patina and seal it with a satin varnish because it blended so well with other pieces of furniture. Scaffolds can be found in various sizes, and if you want to hang yours on the wall for use as a clothes rack, towel rail, or any other practical use you can think of you must consider the height of the ceiling and the proportions of the room.

A PRE-TEEN BEDROOM

Children have definite opinions about how they want their bedrooms to look, especially when they approach their teenage years. This bedroom is not typical – it's neat and clean, for a start! However, it does have some useful reclaimed items, such as the sturdy old school desk that has been painted with a distressed finish, a wall-hung roof-slate blackboard for jotting down homework assignments, wire letter baskets to hold composition books, and a painted wooden window shutter to store the young occupant's CD collection. Another clever storage idea is the pair of wooden ladders (originally one long ladder, cut in half) with zinc shelves set on the rungs. Extra shelves can easily be added as the book collection expands.

SCHOOL DESK

EQUIPMENT

Screwdriver
Clamps
Electric sander
Medium-grit sandpaper
1½-inch paintbrush
Waxing brush or stiff-bristled paintbrush
Soft cotton rags

MATERIALS

Traditional wooden school desk
Wood glue
Wood filler
Dark blue (or desired color) matte acrylic
    paint
Antique brown furniture wax
Matte black acrylic paint

Safety note

Wear safety glasses or goggles when using any
mechanical sanding equipment. Rubber or
protective gloves are also recommended for this
project.

The traditional child's desk, made
of beech and oak and produced
in the thousands for schools
throughout the country, has never
been surpassed for rugged
practicality. These desks have been
replaced, as budgets allow, by
tables or desks often manufactured
in plywood or laminates.

Nowadays, hard-pressed
schools have tight financial
budgets, and many school
custodians spend much of their
time repairing old, graffiti-covered
desks to keep them in use as long
as possible. You may be fortunate
to find a school that has just
received a new shipment of
furniture. If so, there is a chance
that, in return for a small donation
to the school, you will be able to
get a battered – but not
irreparable – desk.

A salvaged solid wood school
desk is well worth the time and
effort required to repair and
refurbish it because it is ideally
suited to a child's bedroom. It
provides useful storage and a
solid surface on which to write,
even in this technology-driven
age. We have given this desk a
distressed paint finish to soften
its appearance.

SCHOOL DESK

METHOD

1 The extent of the damage to the desk will dictate how much repair is needed, but whatever its condition, all metal parts should be removed, and the desk should be taken apart.

2 Inspect all joints for damage, and repair as necessary. Carefully apply wood glue to all joints and reassemble the desk using clamps to secure the joints. Use the electric sander and medium-grit sandpaper to remove all the varnish and most of the graffiti, carved initials, and other childhood markings. Fill any large holes or scratches with wood filler.

3 Paint the exterior of the desk with one coat of dark blue (or desired color) matte acrylic paint. Let the desk dry for at least 24 hours.

4 When the paint is dry, use sandpaper to remove the paint carefully from the edges of the desk where wear would naturally occur. For authenticity, pay particular attention to the corners and legs, where a child's feet would normally cause wear.

5 Use the waxing brush or stiff-bristled paintbrush to apply a liberal application of antique brown furniture wax to a small area, then rub it into the paint with a soft cotton rag. The wax will react with the surface of the paint to create a distressed appearance, and the previously sanded areas will pick up some color from the paint, creating a look of natural wear. Let that area dry and continue working on other areas until the desk is finished. When all the wax is dry, polish with the stiff brush and finish with a clean soft cotton rag.

Paint the inside of the desk with the matte black acrylic paint. It will be almost impossible to remove all the ink stains and other marks on the inside surface, so it is best to paint it black or another dark color.

Reassemble the desk, replacing all the metal parts using the original or similar cross-head screws. The finished desk can be cleaned with a damp cloth and will benefit from an occasional application of clear furniture wax to maintain its appearance.

SLATE BOARD

EQUIPMENT

Paint scraper
Coarse metal file
Coarse-grit sandpaper
Medium- and fine-grade emery cloth
1½-inch paintbrush (optional)
Electric hammer drill
Masonry drill bit
Screwdriver

MATERIALS

Old slate
Satin interior varnish or milk (optional)
Rawlplugs
Two 2-inch screws
Two washers to fit screws (optional)
Chalk or slate pencil

METHOD

1 Select an old slate in relatively good condition with regular edges and nail holes that are not too enlarged. Place the slate on a protected work area and pry off any loose or flaking slate with a paint scraper. Gently tap the surface of the slate with your knuckle; if you hear a hollow sound, more surface slate will have to be removed. Continue until you reveal a solid surface. Use the coarse metal file to clean the edges of the slate and remove any irregularities, always filing toward the edge of the slate.

2 When you have cleaned the slate as best you can with the paint scraper and coarse file, place it on your work area with the bevel-edged side up and use coarse sandpaper to smooth the surface to a rough finish. Complete the process with wet medium-grade emery cloth, followed by fine-grade emery cloth.

Wash the slate with clean water and allow it to dry. If desired, the slate can be painted with one coat of satin interior varnish. Alternatively, follow the old Welsh tradition and apply a thin coat of milk to one surface. When dry, the milk seals the slate and provides an excellent, slightly shiny finish.

3 To fix the slate board to a wall, hold it against the wall in the desired position and mark the screw holes. Drill into the wall with the drill and masonry bit, insert rawlplugs, and fit the slate board to the wall with screws driven through the nail holes into the rawlplugged holes. If the nail holes are a little large, place a washer behind the head of each screw before securing the slate to the wall. Write messages or draw fanciful pictures, whatever you desire, on the finished slate board with chalk or a slate pencil. If you wet the chalk before you use it, the image or writing will stand out much better after it dries.

Safety note

Rubber or protective gloves are recommended for this project.

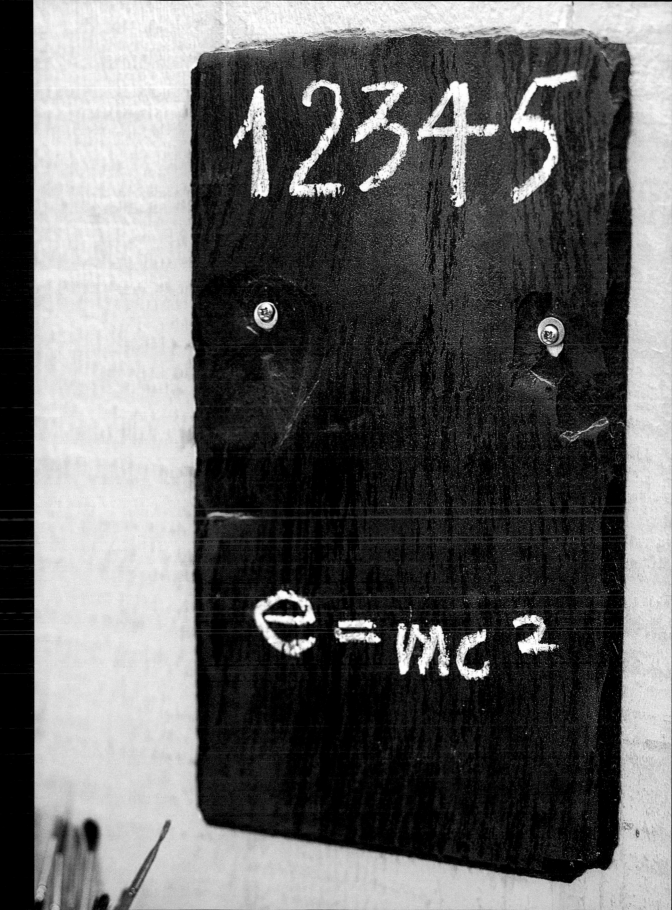

Before the days of inexpensively mass-produced paper, schoolchildren wrote their daily lessons on slate boards. Slate was readily available and economical, and had the added advantage that, after use, it could be wiped clean and used again. In some less-fortunate countries, slate boards are still in use in impoverished schools.

Slate is mined in many parts of the world and ranges in color from almost black, through green and blue, to palest grey. The slate we have used for this stylish wall-mounted board was mined more than 50 years ago and was removed from the roof of a house undergoing restoration. Almost all roofing slates are hand split and shaped to size; the nail holes are generally made at the time the slate is fitted to a roof. All slates, whether old or new, have one flat face and one with a beveled edge.

We have used the existing nail holes in this slate to fit it to the wall. With a little effort, any slate can be easily transformed into an attractive yet functional wall decoration.

STORAGE RACK

EQUIPMENT

Stiff wire brush
Coarse-grade steel wool
Electric hammer drill
Masonry drill bit
Screwdriver

MATERIALS

Galvanized wire letter basket
Four rawlpugs
Four 1½-inch screws

Safety note

Rubber or protective gloves are
recommended for this project.

METHOD

1 Make sure that the basket is dry and remove any remains of protective tape or packaging that might remain on it.

2 Clean the basket thoroughly with the stiff wire brush then finish it with the steel wool to remove any residual oxidation or dirt.

When you are satisfied with the appearance of your basket, hold it up to the wall in the desired position, mark the hanging holes with a pencil, then drill the pencil-marked holes with the electric drill and masonry bit. Insert the rawlplugs before attaching the rack to the wall with the 1½-inch screws.

Here's an easy answer to the constant problem of what to do with books, papers, and all those other items that need to be close at hand but clutter up the surface of a desk or table. A shelf is not always practical and doesn't let you see instantly what you have stored. A wall-mounted rack, however, offers useful storage space for any room in the house.

We located these woven, galvanized wire letter baskets in one of our favorite hunting grounds – a local public auction. Made half a century ago for storing files in garment factory offices, the wire baskets had been stashed away and never installed. They had been stored outdoors, but heavy galvanizing had protected them from years of exposure to the elements. Once we removed the remnants of protective tape and brown paper packaging, they were almost as good as new.

We hope that this project will encourage you to look at unfamiliar objects with an open mind because part of the enjoyment of working with salvaged materials is trying to think of new uses for them. When we first discovered these baskets, we thought that they were too good to pass up although at the time we had no idea of what we were going to do with them. Once cleaned up, they proved to be indispensable in helping to organize our office, the kitchen, and our teenage daughter's bedroom.

SHUTTER CD RACK

EQUIPMENT

Screwdriver
Electric sander
Sandpaper
1½-inch paintbrush
Soft cotton rags
Electric hammer drill
Masonry drill bit

MATERIALS

Old wooden louvered shutter
Colorless wood preservative
Wood filler (if necessary)
Two contrasting colors of matte acrylic
    paint
Satin finish interior wood varnish
Hardboard or thin plywood to fit the back
    of the shutter
Matte black acrylic paint
Small wood screws
Two mirrors
Rawlplugs
Screws to fit mirrors

Safety note

Wear safety glasses or goggles when using any
mechanical sanding equipment. A dust mask
should be worn in case the surface to be sanded
was finished with a lead-based paint. Rubber or
protective gloves are also recommended for this
project.

We know from personal experience that this shutter CD rack is a good idea because it has our teenager's seal of approval. Teenagers usually buy CDs more frequently than the rest of us, and as a collection of CDs expands, storage can become a problem.

Of the innumerable CD storage systems that are commercially available, most take up valuable surface space, and few can be described as well-designed. If, however, you are able to find an old wooden louvered shutter, we are sure you will agree that, once wall mounted at eye level with the CD titles on view, it provides an ideal storage solution.

When selecting an old wooden shutter for conversion into a CD rack, make sure to measure the width of the slats and their distance apart to ensure that the finished rack will comfortably hold boxed CDs. If you wish, you can use the shutter in its original condition and not repaint it, but if you want it to fit into an existing interior decorating scheme, it is probably best to paint it in the color or colors of your choice. We selected an old shutter that showed considerable evidence of age and wear and decided to repaint it in two contrasting colors, completing it with a simulated aged and distressed finish.

SHUTTER CD RACK

METHOD

1 Remove any hinges or other metal hardware, sand down any flaked and loose paint from the shutter, and treat it with the colorless wood preservative. Fill any holes or damage with wood filler, wait for the filler to set, and then sand it down to match the surrounding wood. Sand the entire shutter to provide a smooth surface for the new paint. It is not necessary to remove all the old paint, but pay particular attention to revealing the underlying wood on the edges of the frame and slats, where natural wear would occur.

2 When you are satisfied with the finish, paint the shutter frame in the darker of your selected colors of matte acrylic paint and let it dry. Then paint the slats in the contrasting paler color and let them dry.

3 When the shutter is completely dry, sand through the surface of the paint to reveal the underlying wood on all the outside edges of the frame and the exposed edges of the slats. You can either use an electric sander or, for a more subtle effect, sand by hand. The sanding is designed to simulate natural wear; if you do make a mistake, it is very simple to repaint and start again.

4 When the shutter frame looks suitably distressed, clean off any dust with the cotton rag and apply two coats of the satin finish interior wood varnish to the entire shutter, letting it dry between coats.

Cut the sheet of hardboard or thin plywood to fit approximately ½ inch inside the back of the shutter. Paint one side of the hardboard or thin plywood with the matte black acrylic paint and, when dry, attach it to the back of the shutter with the small wood screws. Fit two mirror hangers to the rear of the shutter and decide where you want to hang it. Drill the holes and insert rawlplugs before screwing the CD rack to the wall.

This fireplace was cast in concrete molded from an old milk churn. It was discovered in the roof of this restored former stable, now a game room, and embellished with the original metal churn handles. The mantle was cut from "green," air-dried oak.

The ideal kitchen these days is very much a living room, sometimes large enough to cook, eat, and socialize in, making it the center of family life. The sitting room and perhaps a

ROOMS FOR LIVING

sunroom are also areas where family and friends can gather for informal entertaining, in tune with the more casual, relaxed lifestyle that many of us now choose.

The decor and the objects we display make a strong statement that reflects our personalities, and with the eclectic nature of decorating today, nothing is totally predictable. Mix surreal combinations of furniture and colors   that is half the fun of decorating. A favorite picture or object that costs next to nothing does not have to be taken too seriously because it injects an individuality and freshness into a scheme that can easily be changed with the next new idea.

Salvage ideas for today's living rooms include vintage office furniture, mass-produced between the 1930s and the 1960s, much of it made of steel or wood or a combination of both to be functional, durable, and well designed. Now, after years of neglect, these pieces are being reclaimed and restored, the dull grey paint covered with vibrant colors to give the furniture a new lease on life, a new purpose, and a place in our homes. Another unconventional idea is to make a base from cheap industrial metal shelving and cover it with piles of huge, sumptuous velvet cushions in rich reds and purples, creating a stylish daybed. These versatile pieces of furniture can be assimilated into any room, mixing comfortably with antiques, at a fraction of the price paid for similar styles from a designer.

In contrast, if you like the warmth of naturally distressed wood, consider using old scaffolding, fencing, floorboards, and farmyard gates to make large dining tables, coffee tables, benches, mirrors, picture frames, and roomy cupboards. This rough-hewn, unrefined furniture celebrates its origins with traces of woodworms, knots, and scores in its often stained, battered, and worn surfaces.

NEAR LEFT

A carved wooden frame, bought from a reclamation yard, then gilded and fitted with glass, makes a superb mirror above a drawing-room fireplace.

BOTTOM RIGHT

A decorative over mantle has been painted and placed above a shelf in a laundry room to deflect the eye from the utilitarian boiler below.

BOTTOM LEFT

The unusual door was cut down and made to fit the opening to what was once the vestry of this converted church. The stone kitchen sink, faucets, and marble-top butcher's slab all came from a reclamation yard. The owner of the church once taught art courses, and the large plate seen behind the faucets was a gift from a ceramics student.

FAR LEFT

Cast-iron nineteenth-century pillars salvaged from a Baptist chapel make an elegant feature installed behind plateglass doors that lead to a flagstone terrace and well-managed garden beyond.

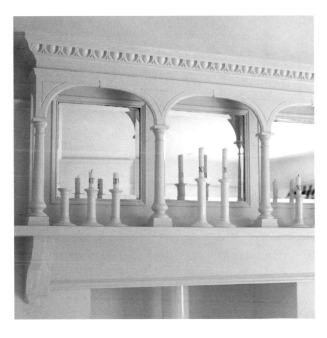

LEFT

The rack above the stove was at one time used to hang cassocks in the vestry, and the Victorian tiles were amassed over a period of 20 to 30 years by the owner of this converted church.

SLATE-TILED WALL

EQUIPMENT

Palette knife
Sandpaper or emery cloth
Tape measure
Diamond-blade electric wet saw
Slate cutter (optional)
2-inch paintbrush
Level
Chalk
Tile adhesive spreader
Soft cotton rags
Fine artist's paintbrush

MATERIALS

Selection of old roofing slates
Black matte acrylic paint
Wall tile adhesive
Satin finish interior or floor varnish

Safety note

Electric cutting equipment can be dangerous.
Most electric tile cutters use water as a coolant
and create a great deal of spray. Wear safety
goggles if you are using an electric cutter; wear
gloves and protective clothes if you use a water-
cooled tile cutter.

Slate, limestone, terra-cotta, and marble are extremely popular natural wall and floor coverings in both home and business environments, despite strong competition from modern man-made high-tech materials.

Hard-wearing slate has long been admired for its beauty as well as its durability. It comes in wonderful shades of red and heather blue as well as the classic dark blue-gray, which seems to go with everything and has always been a favorite material for floors, kitchen countertops, and wall paneling. Mixing slate with limestone, marble, or terra-cotta is very much in vogue. Although they are a fraction of the thickness of traditional flooring slate and have a tendency to flake, reclaimed roofing slates can be used very successfully on floors if laid on a bed of cement to give them a solid base. Floor tiles were often sealed with a coat of milk or oil in the days before prepared sealants became readily available.

Old roofing slates used for this project should be fairly regular in thickness, of similar color, and with two nearly undamaged edges. If the tiles are in particularly good condition, there may be no need to cut them down, but most reclaimed slates have at least one edge that is damaged and enlarged nail holes due to the passage of time and the enthusiasm with which they were removed from the roof.

SLATE-TILED WALL

METHOD

If the slates you will be using for this project are flaking, it is a good idea to pry off the loose layers with a palette knife or similar blade until you have revealed a solid surface. This surface can be cleaned with sandpaper or wet emery cloth to produce a smooth finish.

Measure your tiles and decide on a size into which the tiles can be economically cut. Make sure that the cut slates will not have any unsightly nail holes and that any damaged edges will be trimmed. For simplicity, we chose to cut our slates into squares, which allowed us to cut the slates on the diamond-blade wet saw in only two passes with no need to change the saw fence setting.

Slates cut in this fashion will have two straight cut edges and two of the original naturally beveled edges. For a really professional finish, make the first two cuts of the slate about 1 inch larger than the required dimension, then reduce the saw fence measurement and pass the slates through the saw for a third and fourth time, trimming off the beveled edges to yield four neatly cut edges.

You can cut the slates for this project with a slate cutter (see the Slate Table Mats project in the chapter Wining and Dining), but the resulting edges may not allow the cut slates to be butted neatly together.

1 Measure the area you will be tiling and determine the number of cut slates required. Remember to allow for areas where slates will have to be cut to size or where slate pieces will be needed to complete edges or ends of runs. We also suggest that you cut a number of extra slates to allow for breakage.

Start the diamond-blade wet saw and make sure that the water reservoir is full and that the spinning blade produces a fine spray of water to both lubricate and cool the slate when it is being cut. Set the fence to the desired width, hold the slate firmly in both hands, and, with the true edge against the fence, pass it across the saw table until cut through. Turn the slate 90 degrees and make a second cut at a right angle to the first cut to produce a square slate with two cut and two beveled edges. Repeat until you have as many slates as needed.

2 Carefully mark the area you will be tiling and paint it with one or two coats of the matte black acrylic paint. When the paint is dry, mark the center point on the width of the area to be tiled and, using a level for accuracy, draw a vertical line from the floor to the top of the area with the chalk. Calculate how many horizontal rows of slates will be required to tile the area, halve that number, and multiply by the dimension of the cut slates. Measure down from the top of the area to be tiled by this amount, and at that point draw a horizontal line crossing the vertical line and stretching from one side of the area to the other.

3 Apply wall tile adhesive with the spreader to the back of a slate, then press the slate firmly onto the wall with a gentle twisting movement. Begin with vertical and horizontal rows of slates abutting the chalk marks. Leave the width of a matchstick between the slates. Remove any excess adhesive with a damp cotton rag. For best results, try to fit cut edge against cut edge and beveled edge against beveled edge. When you have fit the slates to the chalk lines, fill in the remaining area with slates, using the first rows as a guide, until the wall is covered. Periodically check your work with the level and tape measure.

4 Use the slate cutter or the diamond-bladed wet saw to trim slates to fit irregular areas and where smaller pieces of slate are required. Use a moist rag to remove any excess adhesive and wipe over the surface of the slates to remove any dirt or dust. When the adhesive is completely dry, use the fine artist's brush dipped in the black matte acrylic paint to touch up the slates or wall as needed. Apply at least two coats of satin finish interior or floor varnish (floor varnish is harder wearing), allowing the wall to dry between coats. Pay particular attention to covering those areas between the slates where the black paint can be seen.

To maintain the appearance of your slate-tiled wall, periodically wipe it with a damp cloth. If the finish deteriorates, it can be restored with another application of varnish.

WAISTED CUPBOARD

EQUIPMENT

Table saw or band saw
Tape measure
Steel square
Hammer
Electric jigsaw
Saucer
Electric sander
Sandpaper
Electric drill and drill bit
Screwdriver
1-inch paintbrush
Waxing brush or stiff-bristled paintbrush
Soft polishing brush
Soft cotton rags

MATERIALS

Waterproof wood glue
1½-inch ring nails
1½-inch paneling nails
1-inch paneling nails
Medium brown wood stain
Four 3-inch screws
Antique brown furniture wax
¾-inch brass screws
Two 2½-inch brass butt hinges
5-inch brass pull handle
1⅝-inch brass turnbutton fastener
1-inch brass screw and washer

Safety note

Protective glasses or goggles are essential if you
are using power cutting equipment, and a dust
mask is advisable. Rubber or protective gloves are
also recommended for this project.

WOOD

For the sides:
Four boards approx. 35 x 4¼ x ½ inch

For the shelves:
Three pieces of floorboard approx.
    8½ x ⅞ inch, one cut to 11 inches and
    two cut to 12 inches

For the back:
Four boards approx. 35 x 3½ x ⅝ inch

For the front:
Two boards approx. 35 x 3½ x ⅝ inch
One top piece approx. 6½ x 3½ x ⅝ inch
One bottom piece approx. 6½ x 5 x ⅝ inch

For the door:
Two boards approx. 24¾ x 3¼ x ⅝ inch
Two braces approx. 6½ x 4 x ⅝ inch
Two pieces approx. 6½ x ⅝ x ⅝ inch

For the top:
Two pieces to equal approx. 15 x 10¼ x 2
    inches

Other:
You will also need a number of pieces of
scrap wood for bracing and supporting the
joints.

If you are looking for furniture
or storage ideas with some
individuality – something a little
different than the mass-produced
designs of today – try making our
rustic-looking "waisted"
cupboard. This highly unusual,
"semi-rough" cupboard can be
made in a variety of sizes, and we
have made a very attractive taller
version. It was constructed using
wooden boards salvaged from
horticulture and produce boxes —
some with the original stencil
markings intact — that were used
before the advent of lightweight
cardboard and plastic containers.
Had the boxes not been rescued,
they would have been used for
firewood.

Select different thicknesses of
wood for the construction: thin for
the sides, without knots (to allow
for uniform bending into the
"waist" shape); thicker for the
doors, front, and back; and
thicker still for the interior shelves.
Any piece of waste wood can be
used for the top of the cupboard,
as long as it is fairly chunky. We
cut our front, door, and sides from
the framework of the boxes, while
the sides were made from the
thinner sides of the boxes. The
shelves were sawed from an old
floorboard, and the top was cut
from two pieces of old floor joist,
glued together to create a piece
the required width. We waxed the
finished cupboard and used
"aged" brass door fittings, but the
cupboard could also be given a
very effective naturally distressed
look and fitted with old steel
hinges, a handle, and turn button.

WAISTED CUPBOARD

METHOD

The waisted cupboard made in this project measures approximately 37 inches high, 15 inches wide, and 10¼ inches deep. All of the measurements can be adjusted to make a different-sized cupboard.

1 Cut the four pieces of wood for the sides of the cupboard, making sure that there are few knots in the boards, and measure three points 3 inches, 16½ inches, and 30 inches from one end (the top). Use the steel square and a pencil to mark lines at these points across the width of the boards. Apply wood glue to the ends of the three shelves and nail them to the side pieces at these points, using the 1½-inch ring nails to hold the joints securely. The 11-inch shelf should be nailed at the 16½-inch point to form the middle shelf.

2 Turn the assembled framework onto its front, keeping the unsawed and naturally colored edge of the shelves facing the front of the cupboard, then, with a pencil, mark a point at the exact center of the width of each shelf. Apply wood glue to approximately the center 7 inches of the rear of each shelf and use 1½-inch paneling nails to secure one of the four back boards to the shelves so that one edge exactly abuts each marked center point. (This will ensure that the curved sides match.) Place a second board abutting and outside the first one, and secure it lightly in place with just one or two 1-inch paneling nails.

3 Attach the third and fourth back boards in the same way to the opposite side of the center marks. Turn the frame over on its back so that the front of the cupboard is up and the newly fitted boards can be seen protruding from the curved edges. With a pencil, trace the edge of the curve on these boards, then turn the frame over, remove the loosely fitted two outside boards, and remove the paneling nails used to hold the boards temporarily in place.

4 Place the two boards that you removed on a solid work surface and cut along the pencil-marked curve with the jigsaw. Apply wood glue to the rear of the shelves and fit the two cut-out back boards in position with 1½-inch paneling nails.

5 Turn the cupboard onto its back and, with a pencil, mark the centers of the shelves on the front. Mark a point 3¼ inches on either side of the center marks on each shelf. Place one of the 35-inch front boards so that it abuts the outside of these points and secure it with one or two 1-inch paneling nails. Turn the cupboard over, mark the curve with a pencil, remove the board, and cut out the shape with the jigsaw. Apply wood glue to the front of the shelves where the board was placed and fit the front board in position, securing it in place with 1½-inch paneling nails. Repeat this step with the second front board.

6 Apply glue to the sides and the exposed edge of the top shelf of the cupboard, then, using 1½-inch paneling nails, attach the 6½-x-3½-x-⅝-inch front top piece between the curved front boards with the front top piece flush with the top of the cupboard. (It may be necessary to support this piece with wood scraps glued and nailed with 1-inch paneling nails behind the curved front boards.) The 6½-x-5-x-⅝-inch front bottom piece should be fitted to the bottom of the cupboard between the curved front boards, supported by wood scraps glued and nailed from behind with 1-inch paneling nails. When the glue has dried, place a saucer or similar circular shape at the base of the fitted bottom piece, draw around the curve with a pencil, and cut it out with the jigsaw.

7 Use the electric sander and sandpaper to smooth all sharp corners and rough wood. Stain any sawed edges with medium brown wood stain, diluted to match the weathered wood. Measure the door space you created and put the cupboard to one side. Take the two 24¾-inch door boards and join them together with the two 6½-inch braces fitted across the rear and fixed with wood glue and 1-inch paneling nails. Take the two 6½-inch pieces of ⅝-inch-square wood, glue one side and fit one each to the top and bottom of the door with 1½-inch paneling nails. This will help to prevent the door from distorting. Place the assembled door in position and shape it with the electric sander to fit it loosely in place.

8 Glue and nail four pieces of wood scrap above the top shelf, inside and flush with the top of the cupboard, to provide a base into which the screws used to fit the top will be fixed. When the glue is dry, apply more wood glue to the top of the wood scrap and place the two pieces forming the top in place, the back flush with the rear of the cupboard and with an equal overhang on each side. Drill four holes through the top into the wood scrap underneath and hold it in place with 3-inch screws.

Use the waxing brush or soft-bristled paintbrush to apply the antique brown furniture wax to the door, top, front, and sides of the cupboard. When the cupboard is dry, polish it with the soft brush and a cotton rag. Use the ¾-inch brass screws to fit the brass hinges to the door, centered 6 inches from the top and bottom. Finally, attach the brass pull handle and the turnbutton fastener outside the door with a 1-inch brass screw and a washer underneath, positioned so that it will secure the door when closed.

CURTAIN ROD AND CURTAINS

EQUIPMENT

Tape measure
Hacksaw or pipe cutter
Paint stripper
Old paintbrush
Wood scraps
Soft cotton rags
Craft knife
Sandpaper
Electric hammer drill
Masonry drill bit
Screwdriver

MATERIALS

Length of 1-inch copper tubing
Approx. 12-inch broom handle
Two tent pole finials or similar decorative
  finials
Wood glue
Four 1-inch brass pipe clamp standoffs
Four rawlplugs
Four 2-inch screws
Clip-on brass curtain rings
Two antique linen sheets

Safety note

Paint stripper is extremely caustic. Wear rubber or protective gloves and eye protection for this project.

It is so simple and inexpensive to make this curtain rod using some old copper piping, two wooden tent pole finials, and a few other bits and pieces that you may decide never to buy one again. Just think of the savings if you were you to make them for the whole house!

Copper piping develops color and patina with age even when the metal is hidden behind layers of paint. It can be bought second-hand from a scrap metal dealer, who probably will charge you for the scrap value only. Copper pipe can be found in various gauges, and we chose 1-inch-diameter pipe, a gauge often used in interior pipe work.

To fix the pipe to the wall, we used pipe clamp standoffs, which are made for the plumbing industry. They are manufactured in two parts: the bracket has two screw holes to allow it to be fixed to the wall, while the outer part that screws into the bracket is comprised of two semicircular holders that secure the pipe. Pipe clamp standoffs are readily available, are inexpensive, and provide a practical alternative to curtain rod brackets.

The metal pipe and wood fittings combine to create the casual, unsophisticated look we desired. We teamed the pole with simple curtains of heavy antique cream linen. Sometimes embroidered with initials in red and occasionally fringed, the curtains were used as sheets in country farmhouses in the early 1900s. Those we used were particularly long and had one embroidered and tasselled end. We chose to highlight this end by folding and hanging the curtains so that the embroidery could be seen.

CURTAIN ROD AND CURTAINS

METHOD

1 Measure the width of the window opening for which the curtain pole is being made. Add approximately 8 inches to the width at each end, then cut the copper tube to that dimension with a pipe cutter or hacksaw. If the pipe is painted, strip the paint with chemical paint stripper, following the manufacturer's instructions carefully and using protective gloves, eye protection, and wearing an apron or old clothes. Lay the pipe on a disposable surface and apply the stripper liberally to the painted surface with an old paintbrush. Leave the area for a short while until the paint blisters, then start to remove the softened paint with a piece of wood scrap. Do not use a metal scraper or anything that is likely to scratch the surface of the pipe and remove the patina that has developed over time. Repeat the process as needed to remove all the paint, wiping the pipe clean with a cotton rag between applications.

2 When the pipe is clean, wash it down with soapy water, dry it with a clean cotton rag, and place it to one side. Cut the broom handle into two halves with the hacksaw. Using the craft knife and sandpaper, shape and sand down one end of one of the pieces until it fits tightly into one of the tent pole finials. Fit the other piece of broom handle into the second finial in the same way. Use the craft knife and sandpaper to shape and sand the other ends; one finial should fit tightly into the pipe, while the other should be sanded so that it is slightly loose and can be easily removed to allow the curtain rings to be fitted over the pipe.

3 Place the completed curtain rod against and above the window in the desired position and mark where the supports should be attached. The supports should be placed at both ends of the rod and just outside the window opening, leaving an approximately 6-inch overhang at each end. Unscrew the pipe clamp standoffs from their brackets, place the brackets at the selected points on the wall, and mark the screw holes with a pencil. Drill holes in the wall at the marked points with the electric drill and masonry bit to a depth of approximately 2 inches, insert the rawlplugs, and fit the pipe clamp standoff brackets with the four 2-inch screws. Unscrew the two semi-circular pipe holders and attach the halves with the threaded attachment to the brackets fixed to the wall.

4 Remove the loose finial from one end of the rod, thread the curtain rings onto it, and replace the finial. Place the rod in the half of the pipe clamp standoffs attached to the brackets and secure the rod in place with the previously removed half-rings. Make sure that the rod is centered on the brackets and that one curtain ring is positioned outside the bracket but inside the finial on each side. Secure the rod in place, tightening the pipe clamp standoffs with the screwdriver.

Fold the antique linen sheets so that, when hung, they will drop to the ground. Divide the curtain rings in half, pushing half to each end of the pole for each curtain and clipping them onto the folded sheets at regular intervals. The last ring on each side, positioned outside the bracket, will keep the curtains spread when they are pulled across the window.

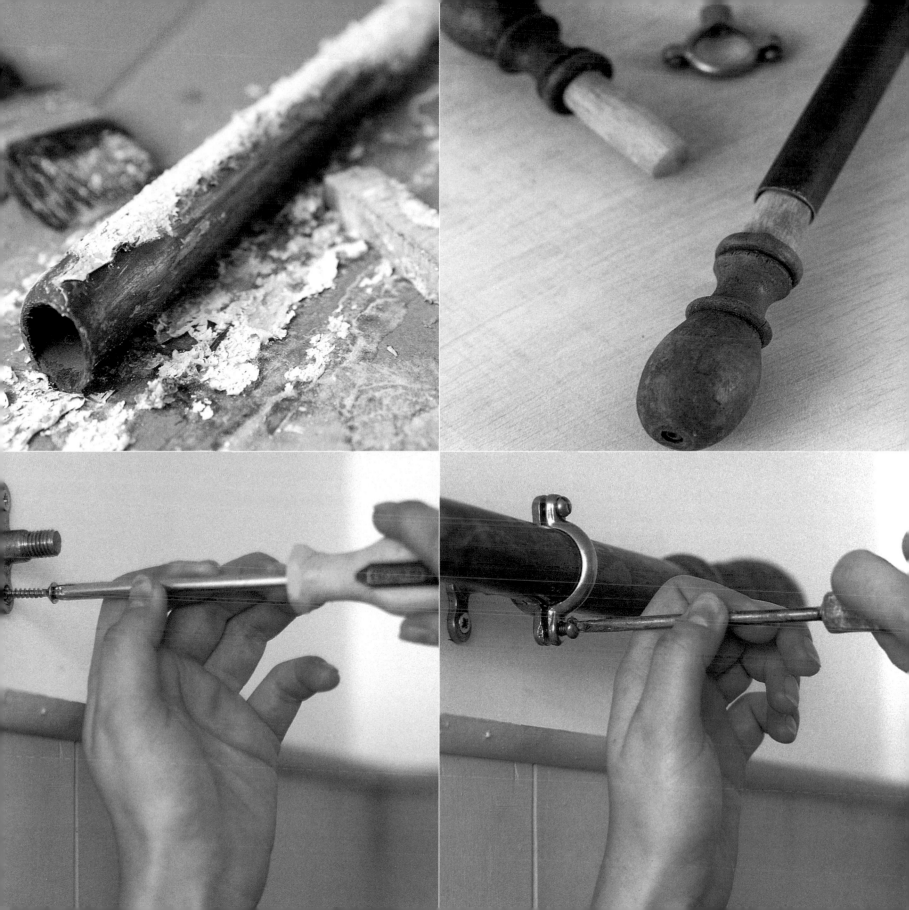

DOCK PILING COFFEE TABLE

EQUIPMENT

Angle grinder and sanding disc attachment
Orbital electric sander
Waxing brush or stiff-bristled paintbrush
Soft cotton rags
Paper towels (optional)

MATERIALS

Three wood blocks
Newspaper or other disposable material
Dark brown furniture wax
Round piece of glass at least ½ inch thick
Glass cleaner

METHOD

1 Select three wooden blocks of similar appearance and height. If the ends are not level, saw or sand them into shape. Place each of the wooden blocks on a flat work surface covered with a disposable material. Use the angle grinder to grind off any surface irregularities and heavy saw marks, and smooth the surfaces with the orbital sander.

2 Apply a liberal quantity of dark brown furniture wax to the sides and top of the blocks with the waxing or stiff-bristled brush. Rub the wax well into the surfaces with soft cotton rags to accentuate the grain and color of the wood; rub off any excess and let the blocks dry. Be careful not to apply any wax to the base of the blocks because the wax will mark the floor when the coffee table is installed.

3 Polish the wood blocks with clean cotton rags, using a new cloth when the first is soiled. For best results, polish in a figure-8 motion, which should leave no smears or marks on the surface of the wood. Make sure you remove any surface wax from the sawed surface of the top of the block because the wax might mark the glass top. Again, check the base of the blocks for any wax residue.

Place the three blocks carefully in the place where you are installing the coffee table. The blocks should be placed an equal distance from each other so that their tops will be approximately 8 inches from the outside edge of the glass when it is placed on top. Clean the glass with glass cleaner, polishing it with more cotton rags or absorbent paper towels, and when you are satisfied with the result, gently place the glass in position on the blocks.

Safety note

When using an angle grinder, wear safety glasses or goggles and a dust mask. A dust mask should always be used when sanding with an electric sander. Rubber or protective gloves are also recommended for this project.

When we first saw these massive wooden blocks cut from the tapered ends of old oak dock pilings, we immediately admired their size and strength. These timbers, lifted from the sea bed, were cut into beams and lintels, leaving behind the tapered ends that we discovered in a local scrap yard.

Years of exposure to salt water had hardened and darkened the oak, which had also been discolored by the iron nails that were used to fix steel caps that once protected the ends of the pilings.

We knew that these hunks of raw timber could be turned into something exciting and innovative, and we decided on a design for a coffee table using the posts for legs. By chance, we came across a huge salvaged round piece of glass, so heavy that it took two men to lift it. The origins of this junk shop find were unknown, but our hunch was that it had previously been used as a table top, suffering remarkably few scratches. The combination of gleaming glass and natural warm, tactile wood gave us exactly the clean architectural lines and interesting contours we had envisioned.

Any wooden blocks could be used to make a similar table, or you may want to construct the legs from terra-cotta pipes, lumps of stone, or even concrete blocks.

DOCK PILING LAMP

EQUIPMENT

Electric drill
½-inch spade or auger bit
Drill bit extension bar
Poker (optional)
Tenon saw
½-inch wood chisel
Hacksaw
Metal file
Palette knife
Electrician's screwdriver
Stiff-bristled brush (optional)
Soft cotton rags (optional)

MATERIALS

Oak post or other large block of wood
12 inches of ⅜-inch threaded brass tubing
Threaded brass lamp holder
Threaded brass adapter (optional)
Two-part epoxy putty
Approx. 8 inches of ⅝-inch copper tubing
Electric plug
Lamp power cord
Brown sealant or filler
Antique brown furniture wax (optional)
Lampshade cradle
Electric light bulb
Lampshade

Safety note

Electricity can be dangerous; we suggest you get a qualified and experienced electrician to check your electrical work on this project.

Rough-hewn and shaped like obelisks, these mighty, metal-braced, oak dock pilings, once driven deep into tidal sands, were a truly exciting discovery. Because of their uniqueness, we felt that they were more than worthy of two different treatments. In this project, one of the dock pilings has been made into a lamp with an Asian flair, with the shade accenting the shape of the rich, dark, heavy base. The other project (the Dock Piling Coffee Table on the previous pages) uses three posts as gargantuan legs for a stylish glass-topped coffee table.

DOCK PILING LAMP

METHOD

1 Place the wooden block on a flat surface, mark the center point on the top surface, and drill a hole to the maximum depth possible, making sure the electric drill is held vertically. Either remove the drill, attach the bit to an extension bar and continue drilling until you have drilled through to the bottom of the block, or turn the block over and drill from the base to meet the hole drilled from the top.

2 Should you choose to drill from each end and the holes do not quite meet, or you need to deepen a drilled hole, you can heat a poker until its tip is red-hot and use it to burn through the remaining wood. This may require several applications of the poker and will create considerable smoke. We suggest that you do this out of doors and make sure that the block does not catch fire. Have some water handy.

3 Use the tenon saw to make two cuts approximately ½ inch apart and ½ inch deep on the base of the block from the center hole to an outside edge. Chisel out the waste to form a groove for the lamp cord. Place the length of $^3/_8$-inch threaded tube in a vice and cut it to length with a hacksaw. Clean the cut end with a metal file and test that it will thread easily onto the lamp holder. Depending on the thread gauges of the tube and lamp holder used, it may be necessary to join them with a threaded brass adapter.

4 Insert the threaded tube into the hole cut through the wooden block, securing it in place with two-part epoxy putty or a similar filler or glue. Make sure that the threaded tube is vertical in the hole and that no putty will prevent the lamp cord being threaded through the tube and through the hole drilled in the block. Use a palette knife to clean the top of the block and scrape away any putty that squeezed out when the tube was inserted, then set the block aside for the putty to harden.

5 Screw the lamp holder onto the threaded tube. Measure from the top of the block to the base of the lamp holder and cut the $^5/_8$-inch copper tube to that length. Unscrew the lamp holder. Attach the electric plug to one end of the lamp cord, place the copper tube over the threaded tube to form a sleeve, then pass the free end of the cord up through the base of the wooden block, through the threaded tube, and out of the top. Fit the cord to the lamp holder with an electrician's screwdriver, then pull it back through the block until the lamp holder sits on top of the tube and copper pipe. Screw the lamp holder back onto the threaded tube, securing the copper pipe sleeve in position.

Use the brown sealant or filler to secure the lamp cord into the groove cut into the base of the block. At this point, the lamp base can be waxed with antique brown furniture wax applied with the stiff-bristled brush, rubbed into the wood with soft cotton rags, and polished off with more rags. Fit a lampshade frame onto the collar of the lamp holder, insert a light bulb, and place the lampshade on the frame.

As we start the new millennium with a softer look, a more gentle kind of minimalism, we use decorative accessories to add impact and interest. Pottery, paintings, porcelain, cushions, worn areas of an old rug can be cut up and backed with burlap material to make enormous floor cushions or wall hangings, and the scraps can be used for smaller cushions.

DECORATIVE ACCESSORIES

rugs, and cherished collections that have evolved over time are the special touches that transform a furnished house into a warm, welcoming, and comfortable home. Not all decorative accessories need be expensive, and when you are bored with something cheap and cheerful, the look can easily be changed.

Textiles bring life and color to a room. Use large throws and rugs in soft, natural shades. The less-

Antique quilt covers, faded linens, silk saris, and fabrics in exquisite colors and textures can be mixed to give a vibrant new look to jaded interiors. Visit garage or yard sales and consignment shops, or raid the attic to find tapestries and beautiful brocades that were once much-loved curtains or gowns that you can cut up to create sumptuous soft furnishings. Salvage old embroideries, braids, trimmings, fringes, and ribbons for added decoration.

Comfortable cushions can be made from old velvet curtains in delicious jewel-like colors with contrast piping, and the same vibrant fabric can be used to recover outdated ottomans, finished off with silk tassels.

Plain walls can be effectively decorated with skillfully hung framed pictures. Old floorboard timbers and unused scaffold boards are obvious materials for mirror or picture frames, and the larger they are, the more dramatic the effect. Do not dismiss the subtle black/brown tar finish of salvaged shiplap boarding, disfigured and rotting former fencing posts, or abandoned farm gates. Even prickly hedgerow twigs, berries, and small boughs, glued together and painstakingly gilded, make the most imaginative of picture frames.

Slate roofing tiles can be cut to suitable sizes to make frames or table mats, and discarded decorative windows, once a source of light and ventilation, can be transformed into unusual and imaginative mirrors. The next time you dig in the garden, collect all those fragments of pretty broken china found buried beneath the surface, and turn them into a mosaic table top, or cover a small shelf, an urn, or a lamp base. A visit to the beach could be the start of a shell or pebble collection that can be used to cover small items like frames or boxes, turning them into intriguing decorative accessories.

All types of metal, from blackened iron curtain poles to gleaming zinc, have been enjoying an upsurge in popularity for the past few years. Metal looks good on its own but mixes equally well with the natural textures of wood, stone, slate, and terra-cotta. It is often used in kitchens and bathrooms because of its hard-wearing and practical qualities, but it should not be excluded from other rooms in the house. Tin plate is an inexpensive alternative to zinc with a strong contemporary look. So hunt out old food tins, which can easily and inexpensively be cleaned up and used to make attractive window boxes.

Books that are read and enjoyed give a home a lived-in, comfortable feel, and vases of freshly cut flowers, admired for their sweet smell as much as their beauty, can fill every room in the house.

LEFT

Hedgerow cuttings have been dried, hot-glued to a wooden frame, sprayed with gesso, and finished with solid gold leaf.

BOTTOM LEFT

Rich velvet curtains have been made into cushions. Enough fabric was left to cover an old ottoman.

FAR LEFT

A mirror made from roofing slates screwed to a plywood base shows how basic materials can be given a new lease on life.

TONGUE-AND-GROOVE CLOCK

EQUIPMENT

Tape measure
Handsaw
Craft knife (optional)
Sandpaper
Miter saw
Electric drill
Drill bit to fit the housing nut on the
    clock shaft
Hammer
Pliers

MATERIALS

Selection of tongue-and-groove boards
Square of ⅜-inch or ½-inch plywood
Wood glue
Scrap wood
1-inch paneling nails
Length of rough-cut wood approx. `
    2 x ½ inch
Battery-powered clock
Battery

METHOD

1 Choose a variety of different colored tongue-and-groove boards similar in size and pattern. Remove the tongue from the boards with a handsaw or craft knife, and finish the edge with sandpaper. To cut the triangular pieces for the clock face, measure the width of the board and make a mark that distance along one length of the board for each two pieces you wish to cut. Cut off one end of the board at the first mark with the miter saw set at the 90-degree setting, move the saw to the 45-degree position and cut out the triangle. When the first triangle is cut, move the saw back to the 90-degree setting, slide the board up to the next mark and continue cutting in the same manner until you have cut the number of triangles required. Repeat with the different colored boards.

2 Arrange the cut triangles on a flat surface until you have created an attractive pattern for your clock face. Measure the outside dimensions and cut a square to that size from the ⅜-inch or ½-inch plywood. Apply wood glue to one side of the plywood and place the triangles on it in your chosen pattern. Put a weight on top of the clock face and set it

aside to dry. When it is fully dry, place the clock face right side up on a piece of scrap wood and drill a hole in the center from the front through the base board and plywood and into the scrap wood underneath. Drilling through the face into the scrap wood minimizes the risk of the hole tearing where the bit emerges.

3 Take the length of rough-cut wood and cut it on the miter saw so it fits as a frame around the clock face. Attach it with the wood glue and the 1-inch paneling nails driven into the plywood edges.

4 Fit the clock housing nut from the front into the hole drilled in the clock face, then insert the clock mechanism from the rear, passing the shaft up through the drilled hole into the housing nut. Attach the clock hands and secure them with the locking nut tightened with pliers. Attach the battery to the back of the clock mechanism, adjust the hands to the correct time, and hang your finished clock. If desired, fit a strut to the back of the clock and use it on a table top.

We admired frames made from recycled cypress tongue-and-groove boards at a furniture trade fair in North Carolina. One exhibitor made a wide range of furniture from salvaged and recycled materials, including rusted corrugated iron, copper sheeting, pine skirting boards, and other discarded wood.

In this project, we show how a simple clock can be constructed from readily available tongue-and-groove boarding.

Tongue-and-groove boarding has been produced in a multitude of sizes and patterns. Modern tongue-and-groove paneling or flooring is generally about 4 inches wide and ¼ inch thick, while older tongue-and-groove boarding can be 6 inches, 8 inches, or even 9 inches wide and is normally ½ inch thick. Various patterns are available, with the most common tongue, groove and, vee, and the most attractive tongue, groove, and bead. When butted together, the tongue of each board fits into the groove of its neighbor, and the vee or bead makes an interesting and uniform feature across the assembled boarding.

Most salvaged tongue-and-groove boards are damaged when they are dismantled, often having the tongue broken off. But since this project calls for the tongue to be removed anyway, damaged tongue-and-groove boards, which can often be purchased quite cheaply, will work just fine.

FENCE FRAME

EQUIPMENT

Tape measure
Steel square
Pencil
Handsaw
Screwdriver
Medium-grit sandpaper
½-inch paintbrush
Glass cleaner
Soft cotton rags or paper towels
Hammer
Electric hammer drill (optional)
Masonry drill bit (optional)

MATERIALS

Two 53-inch lengths of ½-inch-thick fence
   boards, one 3 inches wide and one
   2½ inches wide, selected for color and
   condition
Colorless wood preservative
Wood glue
¾-inch screws
Medium brown wood stain
Glass or mirror glass to fit frame rebate
   (approx 13 x 9 inches)
Hardboard or ¼-inch plywood to fit frame
   rebate
1-inch finishing nails
Two screw eyes or D-rings
Picture hook or screw hook
Nylon picture cord

METHOD

1 Treat the fence boards with the wood preservative. Use the steel square and pencil to mark the 3-inch board into two 18-inch and two 8-inch lengths. Cut the boards at the marks with the handsaw. Selecting the better face of the wood to be the front, place the front face down on a flat surface, with the shorter lengths placed between the longer lengths in the shape of the frame you are constructing.

2 Measure the width of the assembled frame shape. The measurement should be approximately 14 inches. Cut two pieces from the 2½-inch board to this length. Apply wood glue to the back of the assembled frame, then place the new boards over both widths, making sure the outside edges match. Fix each length in place with ¾-inch screws, making sure that they are driven into all three lengths of the underlying boards. Measure the gap between the two newly fitted lengths – the measurement should be approximately 13 inches – and cut two lengths to that size from the remaining 2½-inch fence boards. Fit these lengths into place on the frame, securing them with ¾-inch screws, again ensuring that the outside edges are flush.

3 When the glue is dry, turn the assembled frame over and use sandpaper to remove any sharp edges. Apply the medium brown stain, diluted to match the fence boards, disguising all the exposed newly sawed timber. Cut the glass or mirror glass (or have it cut by a glazier) and the hardboard or plywood backing to fit the frame rebate (approximately 13 x 9 inches). Clean the glass or mirror glass with the cotton rags or paper towels. Place your selected image between the cleaned glass and the backing and insert it into the frame. Secure the backing with the 1-inch finishing nails driven into the sides of the rebate. Alternatively, place the mirror into the frame rebate and secure it in the same way.

Measure approximately one-third down from the top of the frame and insert the screw eyes or D-rings in the center of each side of the frame. Pass the nylon cord through both rings, bring it to the center, and tie it securely with a slip-proof knot. Your frame or mirror is now ready to hang.

Safety note

Always use a wall fixture that can hold the weight of your frame. Smaller frames can be securely hung on single or double picture hooks, which can be driven into most plaster or solid walls; heavier frames will need to be hung on a hook drilled and rawlplugged into the wall.

The wood used to frame this botanical print was taken from old garden fencing that had been dismantled and replaced. After years of battering by high winds, much of the fence had fallen down and some had rotted, but there was still an abundance of good solid wood that was reusable and consequently salvaged. Fencing is usually made from standard softwood, but sometimes cedar, which has a natural resistance to rot, is used. The uneven color comes from exposure to the elements and the effects of lichen and fungi, which attached themselves to the rough surface of the wood over the years.

Whether you are making mirrors or picture frames, consider using reclaimed shiplap boards, old packing cases, or aged pallets, all of which make interesting, unusual, and inexpensive framing materials. The cost of having a number of pictures professionally mounted and framed can be expensive, whereas doing it yourself is much cheaper and more satisfying.

In this project, we demonstrate how to make a frame measuring approximately 18 x 14 inches overall, with an image size of approximately 12 x 8 inches. Obviously, you can construct a frame of almost any size, perhaps to fit a favorite picture or photograph, in which case the measurements must be adjusted accordingly. If desired, you can make this frame as a mirror rather than a picture frame.

LOAF PAN PLANTER

EQUIPMENT

Medium-grade steel wool
½-inch paintbrush
Turpentine for brush cleaning

MATERIALS

Metal loaf pan
Red oxide primer paint
Silver auto spray paint

METHOD

1 Although our loaf pans had been stacked outdoors, the metallic plating was largely intact, except on the sides where it had been exposed to the weather. Rather than strip and polish the whole pan, we decided to treat the rust and refinish the pan with silver metallic paint. There are a number of silver metallic paints currently available, but few accurately simulate a plated finish. The most convincing and effective we found are those produced for the automobile industry, which are available at auto parts stores.

2 Use the medium-grade steel wool to remove the surface rust and reveal a smooth metal surface. Be careful to work along the length of the pan in order to minimize any unsightly scratching.

3 When you are satisfied with the finish you have achieved, use the paintbrush to apply one coat of red oxide paint to both the outside and inside of the pan, and let it dry. Clean the brush with turpentine.

4 Read the manufacturer's directions on the spray paint carefully. Then, following the instructions, spray one coat of paint on the exterior of the pan and approximately 1 inch down the inside. Be careful not to overspray, causing the paint to drip. Put the pan to aside to dry.

When the paint is dry, fill the pan with potting soil and plants. The loaf pan has no drainage holes, so the plants must be watered from the top. Be careful not to overwater the plants, causing the potting soil to become waterlogged.

Safety note

Rubber or protective gloves are recommended for this project. Work on a surface protected with newspaper or other disposable covering. Always use spray paints in a dust-free and well-ventilated area, and be careful not to breathe in fumes; we advise you to use a face mask.

Attractive planters are not always easy to find, but this tin-plated planter filled with pretty flowers or herbs is a wonderful way to smarten up your window sill with a bright, modern look.

The loaf pans we found for this project had apparently been made in the 1960s for a commercial bakery that closed its doors only a few years later. Fortunately, these pans were too large for the average household oven, and we were able to purchase a number of them at an auction at a very good price.

DOORSTOP

EQUIPMENT

Handsaw
Electric drill
⅜-inch spade or auger drill bit
Hacksaw
Small palette knife
Waxing brush or stiff-bristled paintbrush
Soft cotton rags

MATERIALS

8-inch piece of oak molding
Two-part epoxy putty
Wrought-iron handle
Clear furniture wax

METHOD

1 Trim the end of the oak block to size with the handsaw. Place the block on a work surface and drill a hole into the center to approximately half the depth of the block with the electric drill and spade or auger bit. Remove any sawdust or shavings from the drilled hole.

2 Mix the epoxy putty according to the manufacturer's instructions and place it in the drilled hole. Use the hacksaw to cut the handle shaft to fit the block, then insert it into the filled hole. Make sure that the handle is standing upright and, using the palette knife, remove any excess putty that has squeezed out. Set the doorstop aside until the putty sets.

Apply a coat of the clear furniture wax to the top, sides, and end (but not the bottom) of the block with the waxing brush or stiff-bristled paintbrush and rub it into the wood with a soft cotton rag. When the block is dry, polish it with another clean cotton rag.

Unpretentious, this golden oak doorstop with a timeworn iron door bolt handle has plenty of rustic charm. The chunky "green" oak molded ceiling beam from which it was cut came from a restored eighteenth-century home, and the rusty iron door bolt handle was found in our neglected farmhouse kitchen garden. The individual components of the doorstop are unexciting, but, when assembled, the finished doorstop is quite charming. A variety of salvaged items can be used to make similar doorstops, and by using epoxy putty, which provides a very strong hold, you can use many different materials. Consider using a nicely rounded stone or large rock found during a day's beachcombing. Use any object that has enough weight to hold a door open when spring breezes whip through open windows, blowing the curtains and scattering the cobwebs.

WINDOW MIRROR

EQUIPMENT

Stiff-bristled paintbrush
Paint stripper
Paint scraper
Wire brush (metal)
Medium-grit sandpaper (wood)
Small stiff brush (an old toothbrush is
    perfect)
Soft cotton rags
Soft-bristled toothbrush
Tape measure
Straight edge
Wax pencil or felt-tipped marker (to mark
    glass)
Glass cutter
Caulking gun (metal)
Light glazing hammer (wood)
Putty knife (wood)
Pliers

MATERIALS

Clear furniture wax
Antique brown furniture wax (wood)
$\frac{1}{16}$-inch or $\frac{3}{16}$-inch mirror glass
Brown construction adhesive (metal)
Glazing putty (wood)
Glazing pins (wood)
Screw eyes or fitting lugs (metal)
Heavy-duty picture wire
Pair of mirror plates (wood)

NOTE

For metal-framed windows you need all the
equipment and materials listed except for
those marked "(wood)." For wooden-framed
windows you need all the equipment and
materials listed except for those marked
"(metal)."

Safety note

Be careful when using paint stripper or working
with glass: most paint strippers are caustic and
glass can splinter. Always wear safety goggles
and rubber or protective gloves.

Windows have been made in a
multitude of shapes and sizes,
and many can be converted into
stunning ornamental mirrors.
Removed when frames have
rotted or houses are being
updated, arched or decoratively
shaped windows can be found at
architectural reclamation yards,
awaiting transformation into a
beautiful mirror.

Before you start working on
any frame, think about how you
will hang the mirror when it is
completed. Is there somewhere
on the back side where picture
wire can be attached? Can it be
drilled to accept screw eyes, or
do you need lugs welded to the
back? Every window offers a
different challenge. If you are
using a wooden frame, can the
original fittings be removed
without damaging the frame? It is
worthwhile thinking through the
project before you start. For this
project, we have selected a cast-
iron window saved from an
abandoned church. The window is
irregular in shape with no two
panes the same size, which adds
to the visual interest of the mirror
and justifies the extra effort
needed to complete the project.

We have chosen to preserve
the aged and pitted appearance
of the cast iron on our project
mirror, but it could just as easily
be painted, gilded, or given a
distressed finish to add to its
romantic appeal.

WINDOW MIRROR

METHOD

Note that different methods are given for wooden window frames. Read the instructions thoroughly before you begin to ensure that you use the correct method.

1 Clean the window frame with the stiff-bristled paintbrush and then remove all the paint with the paint stripper, being careful to follow the manufacturer's instructions because paint stripper is caustic. (We suggest you use a paint-stripping service, which uses a hot caustic dip system that will loosen any glass and putty still present in the frame.) Remove any glass. If you are using a frame with old glass be careful not to break it. Set the glass aside. Using a paint scraper and wire brush, clean any residual paint and putty from the frame, paying particular attention to the glass rebate. (For wooden frames, use sandpaper instead of a wire brush.)

2 Make sure that the frame is dry and free of any dust or dirt. Apply clear furniture wax to the front of the frame with the small stiff brush, being careful not to get any wax into the glass rebate. Finish with a soft cotton rag. (For wooden frames, wax both front and back, using an antique wax if preferred.) When the wax is dry, polish with the soft brush or a soft cotton rag.

3 Carefully measure the glass rebate, then mark and cut the mirror glass to the exact size. (If you don't want to cut the glass, a glazier will cut the glass to size for you.) Note that $\frac{1}{16}$-inch mirror glass is easier to cut than $\frac{3}{16}$-inch glass and is more suitable for smaller panes. (Because of the small panes in the window selected for this project, we managed to use mirror glass scraps; we numbered each pane as it was cut to ensure a good fit when assembled.) Using the caulking gun, place a very small bead of the construction adhesive inside each frame rebate and fit the mirror glass, pressing it firmly into place. Apply the construction adhesive carefully around the back of the glass to secure it in place. Repeat until all the panes are filled. (For wooden frames, fill the glass rebate with softened glazing putty and fit the glass in place. Use the glazing hammer and glazing pins to secure the glass. Fill the remaining rebate with putty and finish to a beveled edge with the putty knife.)

Remove any excess construction adhesive from the mirror surfaces and let it set. Feed the heavy-duty picture wire through the lugs, screw eyes, or plates on the back of the frame and tie it in place. Use slip-proof knots and tighten the wire with pliers, tying any excess wire to the lugs. Cast-iron frames are extremely heavy, so make sure that the wire used is strong enough to hold the frame and that the knots used are slip-proof. Caution: When hanging the mirror, make sure that the fixtures used will carry the weight of the mirror. Use rawlplugs and screws rather than picture hooks.

TRICK OF THE TRADE

Modern glass is produced by a "float" process and is free of any blemishes or irregularities; old glass, however, is often full of imperfections, which add to its charm. If you prefer your mirror to have an antique appearance, fit the new mirror glass behind refitted salvaged glass panes or glass cut from an old sheet. Make sure that the window rebate is deep enough to hold both sheets of glass and that the old glass and new mirror are clean before you fit them.

The next few pages are filled with
a stunning array of shape and
form, all united by one thing in
common: illumination. These
lighting-design ideas range
from glamorous, fragile-looking

LIGHT AND SHADE

chandeliers to lamps made
from humble roofing tiles. We
take lighting for granted, simply
stretching out an arm to turn
on a light switch or pushing a
button on the remote control.
All it takes, however, is an
unexpected power outage to
throw us into panic and a frantic
search for matches and candles,
which usually turn up the
moment power is restored!

It seems strange to think that
less than 100 years ago many
houses, especially in rural areas,
had no electricity and that people
relied on gas lamps and candles
to complete daily chores and
tasks as well as reading, sewing,
and other leisure activities.
In contrast, today we have a
large variety of lighting choices,
including unobtrusive recessed
lighting, washes of light to accent
interior details, and dimmer
switches that can swiftly change
the mood of a room.

ABOVE

Clear and colored plastic knives, forks, and spoons have been used to create this eye-catching chandelier. An empty sunflower oil bottle covers the center of the chandelier, while others have been cut down to make the candle cups. Fake candles have been made from cardboard tubes.

RIGHT

This chandelier was created using a fantastic variety of salvaged materials including bread racks, Pyrex cups, glasses, metal chains, and pastry tins bought at thrift shops and flea markets.

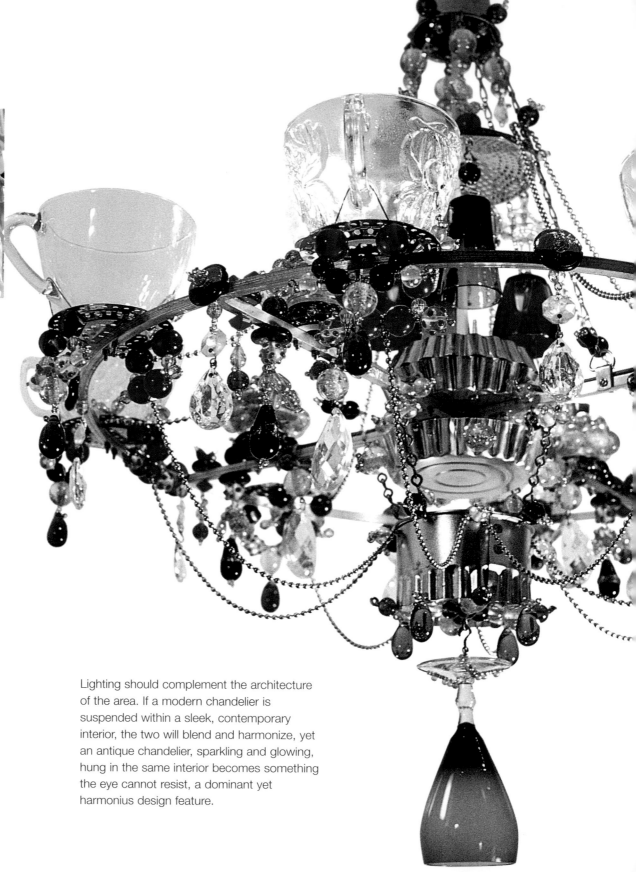

Lighting should complement the architecture of the area. If a modern chandelier is suspended within a sleek, contemporary interior, the two will blend and harmonize, yet an antique chandelier, sparkling and glowing, hung in the same interior becomes something the eye cannot resist, a dominant yet harmonius design feature.

LEFT

A bulb has been placed under an iron pavement grill, radiating an arc of filtered light onto the wall above.

BOTTOM LEFT

This double Roman terra-cotta roof tile has been secured to the wall to create an unusual, robust, and practical rustic light fixture.

BOTTOM RIGHT

This pillar lamp was designed and made from thinly cut and painstakingly joined pieces of end-grain softwood cut from pallets to give a soft, filtered light.

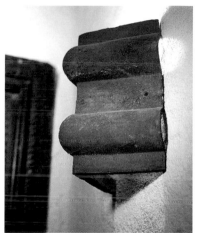

When searching for objects that can be given a new life as something different than their original use, we found that if no other idea came to mind, our discovery could always become yet another lamp or candle holder. The stainless-steel drum of a washing machine made a perfect ceiling light fitting, and the gnarled oak blocks cut from dock pilings became not only the legs of a glass-topped coffee table (see page 74) but also a charming table lamp base (see page 78). Another striking lamp base was made from a large glass carboy (see page 108) once used to transport glucose, while the rusty old metal hoops from an oak pickle barrel and a chain found buried under a pile of discarded agricultural equipment were transformed into a simple but eye-catching candlelit chandelier (see page 100).

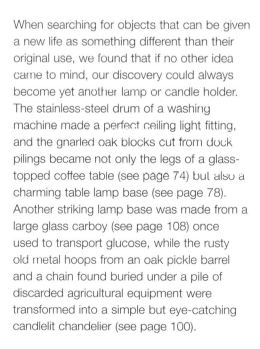

In the chapter Wining and Dining, a heavy metal flower display stand bought at auction was re-created as a decorative candle stand (see page 22). Ordinary rusty bedsprings were transformed into a real conversation piece — a contemporary-looking centerpiece for the table (see page 122). Finally, wooden staircase newel posts, each drilled at one end to hold a giant candle, became imposing candle stands (see page 126).

HOOP CHANDELIER

EQUIPMENT

Wire brush
Palette knife
Sandpaper
Electric drill and selection of wood bits
Screwdriver
½-inch paintbrush
Old toothbrush
Soft polishing brush
Soft cotton rags
Hacksaw

MATERIALS

Two barrel hoops of slightly different
    diameters
Wood scraps
Two-part wood filler
Four mop- or broom-head holders
Eight ¾-inch screws
Four 1½-inch cup hooks
Four 1½-inch screw eyes
Four steel marlin spikes
Four split rings
Four small lanyard hooks
Black satin finish stove paint
Black stove polish
Ceiling hook
Approx. 8 feet sturdy metal chain
Candles

Safety notes

Lit candles are a fire hazard, so always hang your
chandelier far enough from the ceiling to ensure
that there is no danger of fire or smoke damage.
Rubber or protective gloves are recommended for
this project. Make sure that all fixtures are secure
and that the chandelier is fastened into a ceiling
joist or other structural timber. Under no
circumstances should it be attached to laths,
plaster, or plasterboard.

Suspended from the ceiling, this simple but heavy metal design, which evolved from mostly industrial components offers a sharp contrast to the delicate appearance of some of our other chandeliers.

As old oak whiskey barrels or smaller pickle barrels used as garden planters finally give way to rot, remember to salvage the metal hoops. The cooper used these hoops of graduated sizes to secure the shaped wooden laths in place. To make this chandelier you will need to select two hoops of slightly different diameters. (Alternatively, you could use a wooden wheel for the frame, or, if you have access to welding equipment, a metal wheel.)

You will also need old-fashioned metal mop-head holders to make candle holders and a number of heavy steel marlin spikes to dangle underneath. These weighty drops are not just decorative. They help to keep the chandelier level, compensating for any differences in weight across the frame of the chandelier, and stable, preventing it from swinging in inevitable drafts. The marlin spikes could be replaced with any other heavy item that could be attached to the screw eyes.

The hoops came from our garden, the mop-head fittings were discovered in a recycling yard, and the steel marlin spikes were sold to us by a local welder. All the other fittings came from hardware shops. The sturdy chain, which was absolutely essential to hold the weight of the finished chandelier, was part of a lot bought at a farm sale.

HOOP CHANDELIER

METHOD

1 Clean the barrel hoops with the wire brush to remove surface rust and grime. Place them on a work surface, one inside the other, and use scraps of wood to wedge the hoops apart so that a consistent gap is created between the hoops around their circumference. Fill the gap with two-part wood filler (any other plasticized filler that can be drilled and will hold a screw securely is an acceptable alternative) and smooth it with the palette knife.

2 Turn the joined hoops over and fill the gap with more filler. When the filler has cured, finish with sandpaper. Mark four equally spaced points on one surface of the filled and joined hoops and place a mop-head holder on each. Mark the points on the wood filler where the mop-head holders will be attached, remove the holders, and drill holes to accept the ¾-inch screws. Attach the four mop-head holders with screws inserted into the filler.

3 Mark four points on the same side of the joined hoops midway between each mop-head holder, then drill holes for and attach the four cup hooks. Turn the joined hoops over and drill four holes under the mop-head holders, and attach the screw eyes. (For added strength, the screw eyes and cup hooks can be screwed into the filler before it has fully cured; otherwise, coat their threads with filler before fitting them into the drilled holes.)

4 Paint the the cup hooks, screw eyes, and mop-head holders, together with the marlin spikes, split rings, and lanyard hooks, which are not yet attached to the chandelier, with black satin finish stove paint and let them dry. When they are fully dry, take the old toothbrush, dip it into the black stove polish and paint over the chandelier and fittings. When they are dry, polish them to a light sheen with the soft brush and clean cotton rags.

5 Fix the ceiling hook securely to a roof joist or other structural timber above where your chandelier will hang; because of its weight, under no circumstances should it be fitted to laths, plaster, or plasterboard. Decide how far you want it to hang from the ceiling and cut the chain into two lengths, each double that measurement. Place the ends of each chain over opposing cup hooks and the center of the chains onto the ceiling hook. Fit split rings and lanyard hooks to the marlin spikes and hang the spikes from the screw eyes on the chandelier. Finally, insert candles into the mop-head holders and your chandelier is complete.

HIP TILE CEILING LAMP SHADE

EQUIPMENT

Wire brush
Electric hammer drill
Masonry drill bit
Metal snips
Empty caulking gun
Dry sand or gravel
Metal or strong plastic bucket
Hacksaw
Pliers

MATERIALS

Three clay hip tiles
Waste copper or aluminum sheet
Construction adhesive
Metal chain
Metal wire
Ceiling hook

SAFETY NOTE

This ceiling lamp shade is extremely heavy, so make sure that all fittings are secure and that the ceiling hook is fastened into a ceiling joist or other structural timber. Under no circumstances should it be fitted to laths, plaster, or plasterboard.

We have always enjoyed the warmth and traditional look of terra-cotta tile and have searched for different ways to use and enjoy this natural material.

Weathered roof tiles are particularly attractive, with lichen and water stains adding to their character. We used reclaimed hip tiles for this project. Hip tiles are used to cap the joint, or "hip," of a roof, and innumerable patterns are available.

Terra-cotta roof tiles used as wall lights are a familiar sight in Spain and other Mediterranean countries, and we show you how to make one in the chapter Design and Detail (see page 130).

You may choose to construct your ceiling lamp shade with the opening downward rather than upward, as ours is made, but whichever way you choose, the shade is heavy and must be hung on a chain fixed to a strong hook driven through the plaster and into a ceiling joist.

In our travels, we have seen hanging lights created from terra-cotta flower pots hung upside down and suspended from a ceiling. Particularly striking was a seaside villa in Italy, where clear wine bottles in groups of eight or ten, each with a light inside, provided illumination. We've also seen a wooden grain hopper used to make a shade for a light in a high-ceilinged sitting room in a vacation home that was formerly a corn mill.

HIP TILE CEILING LAMP SHADE

METHOD

1 Select three hip tiles that are of equal size and relatively undamaged. Using the wire brush, clean off any lichen, dust, or dirt from their surfaces, paying particular attention to the inside (or concave) surfaces. With the electric drill and masonry bit, drill a hole in the center of the splayed end of each tile. Drill from the outside (or convex) side to prevent unsightly flaking of the clay surface where the drill bit emerges.

2 Use the metal snips to cut the waste copper or aluminum sheet into three strips, each approximately 4 inches wide and the length of the tiles. Place two tiles together, concave sides up and supported by wooden blocks or spare tiles so that the edges fit tightly together, and, using the caulking gun, apply a liberal quantity of construction adhesive to the full length of both tiles, approximately 2 inches from both sides of the joint. Press one cut copper or aluminum strip onto the adhesive and press down to make a secure joint.

3 Place the dry sand or gravel into the bucket to support the tiles, and then gently place the joined tiles into the bucket, pointed end down. Place the third tile in the bucket to make a tightly fitting cone shape of three tiles. You may have to add or remove sand or gravel to support the tiles properly in the bucket. When you are satisfied with the arrangement, apply construction adhesive approximately 2 inches from both sides of the two remaining joints and secure with the copper or aluminum strips. Make sure that the metal strips are securely bonded to the adhesive, then let the tiles set for at least 24 hours or until the adhesive has cured.

Remove the tiles from the bucket and clean off any residual adhesive. Measure three lengths of chain slightly longer than the height at which you want to hang the finished light from the ceiling and cut them to length with the hacksaw. Fit the chain lengths to the drilled holes in the tiles with the metal wire and secure the wire with the pliers. Use the pliers to make sure that the chain is securely fitted. Hang the finished lamp shade from the chains fitted to a hook driven into a ceiling joist.

CARBOY LAMP

EQUIPMENT

Electric drill
1¼-inch plug cutter (to fit inside the bottle
    top)
Sandpaper
Multi-speed electrical tool and sanding
    head (optional)
¾-inch auger or spade drill bit
Round wood file
Wood filler or two-part filling compound
    (optional)
Hammer
Glass cleaner
Cotton rags or absorbent paper towels
Electrician's screwdriver

MATERIALS

Piece of 2-inch-thick wood (preferably
    softwood)
Glass carboy bottle
Bottle lamp holder with side fitting and
    adjustable stem and electric power cord
    attached
Lamp holder
Lampshade
60 watt electric light bulb
Electric plug

METHOD

1 Use the 1¼-inch plug cutter to cut a plug out of the piece of 2-inch-thick wood. You will have to measure the diameter of the inside of the top of the bottle you are using and cut a plug slightly larger than that measurement. Use sandpaper or the multi-speed electrical tool and sanding head to sand the plug down to a lightly tapered shape until it will fit tightly inside the top of the bottle.

2 Use the electric drill and auger or spade bit, placed in the hole already cut in the center of the plug, to cut a second hole, ¾ inch in diameter, in the plug. Again, this measurement depends on the bottle lamp holder you are using. Most are made from plastic, and the stem is designed to compress to fit differing hole sizes, so adjust the size of your hole to fit. If necessary, enlarge this hole to fit the lamp holder stem with the round wood file or multi-speed electrical tool and sanding head.

3 Gently insert the stem of the lamp holder inside the plug so that it is securely held. If the lamp holder is loose, you can use the wood filler or two-part filling compound to fix it in place.

Clean the inside of the bottle because once the lamp holder is inserted you will not be able to clean it. A simple way to remove stains from the inside of a glass container is to fill the container with a small amount of sharp gravel and shake it vigorously. Shake out the gravel, rinse the container with hot soapy water, and let it drain.

4 Carefully place the wooden plug and lamp holder into the top of the bottle; it should be a tight fit. Tap the plug home into the bottle using a hammer cushioned with a scrap of wood, gently working around the circumference of the plug. If the plug is too tight a fit, you may break the bottle as the plug is driven home, so err on the side of caution and remove the plug and lamp holder, sand off a little more wood, and try it again until the plug fits securely inside the neck of the bottle.

Clean the outside of the bottle with the glass cleaner and polish it with the cotton rag or absorbent paper towels. Unscrew the top of the lamp holder and attach the shade holder and the lampshade. Insert the light bulb and attach the electric plug to the power cord attached to the lamp holder.

Safety note

Electricity can be dangerous; we advise that all electric fittings be checked by a qualified electrician.

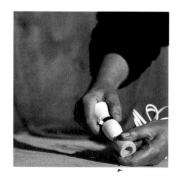

Hand-blown glass has an enduring appeal. It is strong and fluid yet fragile and delicate, with light dancing off its shape, reflecting the colors of the room surrounding it. The carboy we selected as a lamp base is a utilitarian clear glass bottle that was originally designed to transport large quantities of glucose for use in the wine-making trade. It was protected by a wooden cradle while in transit. Since glass resists corrosion, carboys were also used to transport acid. No two carboys are identical, differing slightly in their overall shape and look – they can sometimes be found in a glorious green hue with bubbles embedded in the glass.

At one time, these bottles filled with brightly colored liquids were seen in the front window of every respectable pharmacy. If one could buy them, they would be converted into superb lamps. Since fashion is cyclical, we have recreated this style with our Carboy Lamp.

GLOBE LIGHT

EQUIPMENT

Electric drill
½-inch auger or spade drill bit
Tenon saw
High-speed multipurpose tool with saw
    attachment (optional)
½-inch wood chisel
Soft cotton rags
Electrician's screwdriver

MATERIALS

Wooden tent pole base plate (or similar
    round piece of wood)
Medium brown furniture wax
¾-inch screws
Water-based wood glue
Green felt
Rubberized glue
Glass globe

ELECTRICAL

Approx. 2 yards electric power cord
Metal or plastic flat-based lamp holder
Electric plug
Electric light bulb (60 watt maximum)

Safety note

Electricity can be
dangerous; we advise
that all electric fittings
be checked by a
qualified electrician.

METHOD

1 Take the tent pole base plate and drill through the center from the top with the ½-inch auger or spade bit. Place the base plate on a piece of scrap wood, unless your work surface can withstand the drill bit passing into it. (If you are using a round piece of wood with no indented area, you must drill or cut a rebate in the top large enough to house the globe glass light comfortably.)

2 Turn the wooden base over so that the bottom faces upward and, with a tenon saw, make two cuts approximately ½ inch apart and ½ inch deep leading from the drilled center hole to the outside edge. (A high-speed multipurpose tool with saw attachment will speed up this step.) Use the ½-inch wood chisel to remove the wood between the saw cuts to leave a groove for the electric power cord.

3 Apply a liberal amount of medium brown furniture wax to the top and sides of the base, rubbing it well into the wood with a clean cotton rag. Make sure you don't get any wax on the bottom surface of the base. Let the wax dry and be absorbed into the wood, then polish the base with another clean rag. A second application of wax will improve the finish.

4 Pass the electric power cord up through the center of the wooden base and, with the electrician's screwdriver, fit it to the flat-based lamp holder. Screw the lamp holder to the bottom of the rebate in the base with the ¾-inch screws. Fit the electric plug to the other end, pull the cord taut, and secure it into the groove cut in the bottom of the base with the water-based wood glue. Let the glue dry.
    When the glue has dried, cut the felt to fit the shape of the bottom of the lamp base and attach it in place with the rubberized glue. When the glue has dried, insert an electric light bulb into the lamp holder and place the glass globe light over the top of the bulb.

To make this simple but effective light, with its soft, unobtrusive glow, you need only three main components: a base, a glass globe, and the electrical parts.

In our constant search for salvaged materials, we often turn to our friendly scrap dealer. We know from experience that after a couple of hours at his yard, we will leave full of inspiration and, fortunately for him, with several purchases. Clambering into the back of a smelly old shipping container used as storage in the yard, we saw rows of round pieces of wood that resembled farmhouse cheeses lined up in a dairy.

We were unable to guess their origin, but the scrap yard owner enlightened us — they were the turned ash or beech pole base plates used to stop the poles of old canvas tents from sinking into soft ground. After many years of service, the canvas tents were either passed on to the Boy Scouts or donated to charities, which distributed them as emergency relief shelters to disaster areas worldwide (minus their wooden feet). The tents that were in too poor a condition to use were thrown away, and all that was left behind were the tent poles, pole bases, and guy rope pegs we discovered on our visit.

Spherical glass — opalescent, clear or sometimes patterned — can be found in different sizes at architectural reclamation yards. The owner of our favorite salvage yard told us that our glass globes were once the enclosed covers for bathroom lights.

COLUMN LAMP

EQUIPMENT

Electric planer or hand plane
Combination square
Clamps
Medium-grit sandpaper
Sanding block
Tape measure
Pencil
Compass made from string, pencil, and
    tack or nail
Jigsaw and fine wood-cutting blade
Electric drill
½-inch spade drill bit
Straight edge
Handsaw
Soft cotton rags
Hammer
½-inch wood chisel or craft knife
Waxing brush or stiff-bristled paintbrush
Paste brush
Electrician's screwdriver

MATERIALS

The project lamp has been designed as
a table lamp, but all dimensions are
approximate and can be adjusted for the
materials available and the size of the lamp,
which may be scaled up or down.

Approx. 2 yards of 8-x-2-inch salvaged
    softwood joists
Wood glue
Furniture wax polish
Approx. 9 yards of ¾-x-⅜-inch planed dowel,
    cut into twelve 30-inch lengths
Tissue or other translucent paper
    (handmade paper is an alternative)
Wallpaper paste

ELECTRICAL

Electric plug
Electrical power cord
Plastic lamp holder
Electric light bulb (60 watt maximum)

Safety note

Electricity can be dangerous; we advise that all
electric fittings be checked by a qualified
electrician.

The vertical beam of light thrown
by the hole in the top of the
column and the muted illumination
shining through the wooden
beading and tissue paper used in
its construction give this light an
Eastern feel.

Salvage designers have
created lamps using everything
from lead, old terra-cotta land
drains rescued after almost 200
years underground, ancient oak
and elm lumber, and even glass
salvaged from the cockpit of a
dismantled airplane. They have
worked with other recycled
materials, including stone, metal,
and glass, interpreting designs,
making and restoring furniture,
and undertaking a variety of
construction and restoration
projects around the world.

This column lamp can be made
in various sizes, from hardwood or
softwood. For this project, we
have selected wood cut from old
softwood joists for the base and
column construction and salvaged
beading board to form the
column. Old brass stair rods
would also make unusual
connectors.

COLUMN LAMP

METHOD

1 Cut the 8-x-2-inch softwood joists into four 12-inch lengths and two 15-inch lengths. Plane one edge of each cut length, using the combination square to make sure it is square. Take two pieces of each cut length and, using the glue and clamps, join them together planed edge to planed edge. Repeat with the remaining lengths until you have two pieces of wood 16 x 12 inches and one 16 x 15 inches. Let them dry for at least 24 hours before removing the clamps. When the glue is dry, plane the faces of the wood pieces and use the sandpaper and sanding block to finish.

Using the pencil, mark a point at the center of one face of the 15-inch joined length of wood. Take a piece of string and tie one end to the tack or nail placed firmly on the center mark on the wood and tie a pencil to the other end of the string, 7 inches from the center, to make a simple compass. Holding the tack or nail in one hand and the pencil in the other hand, draw a 14-inch circle on the board to create the outline of the lamp base and then set the board aside. Shorten the string to 5½ inches and draw circles 11 inches in diameter on both 12-inch joined lengths of wood to create outlines for the column base and top. Shorten the string to 3 inches and, using the same center points, draw two additional circles 6 inches in diameter inside the 11-inch drawn circles on the wood.

2 Using the jigsaw, cut carefully around the rings to make three circular boards, one 14 inches and two 11 inches in diameter. Cut ½-inch holes in the centers of all three boards with the electric drill and spade bit. Take the 14-inch board (lamp base) and, on the underside starting at the drilled center hole, draw two lines ½ inch apart with a pencil to the outside edge. Use the handsaw to cut along the pencil lines to a depth of approximately ⅜ inch, then remove the waste wood with the wood chisel to create a channel for the electric power cord. Cut out 6-inch centers in the 11-inch column base and top, using the drilled hole for jigsaw blade access. Smooth the exposed sawed edges with the sandpaper.

3 Depending on the final appearance desired, wax and polish the column base and top and lamp base with the soft rag to the desired finish. Take the column base and top and, with the drill and spade bit, cut 12 equally spaced holes around the outside of both boards approximately ¾ inch from the outside edge and approximately ½ inch deep. Ensure that the 30-inch lengths of the rectangular wooden dowel are free from knots or bends, and trim the ends with a chisel or craft knife to fit tightly into ½-inch holes. Drive these 12 dowels into the drilled holes to join the column base and top, and secure with wood glue. Let the lamp frame dry.

4 Take a number of approximately 1-yard torn lengths of your selected paper, apply wallpaper paste to one side, then carefully stretch the lengths of paper around the lamp and over the dowels. When the dowels are covered to your satisfaction (several layers of paper may be required), let the paper dry. You have now completed the construction of your lamp.

Attach the plug to one end of the electric power cord. Feed the other end of the cord from the underside of the lamp base through the drilled hole and attach it to the plastic lamp holder that has been screwed to the top of the base over the hole. Place the light bulb in the lamp holder and then place the assembled column on top.

In this chapter, we offer a number of designs that are not only functional but also visually interesting. Even when a design has been specially commissioned, it can be quite

Where companies or individuals have conscientiously worked to salvage and reuse materials, the end results can be superb. Handmade clay bricks have a wonderful depth of color, and

DESIGN AND DETAIL

a challenge to make it work in a practical sense, and when the item or product is old and has been made for an entirely different use or situation, the challenge is that much greater. Of course, the easy way out is to buy "off the shelf," rather than consider how something might be adapted for reuse. But finding a solution is half the fun!

even the heavy bricks rescued from crumbling fireplaces — indoors and outdoors — or from the scrap heap make stunning entryway or kitchen floors. Roof slates, laid on concrete, their nail holes filled with lead and highly polished, also can be transfigured into a floor of great beauty that seems to stretch to infinity.

ABOVE LEFT

Solid mahogany doors, rescued from a crumbling bank building, divide the entrance hall in this house from a more formal inner hall. The gold leaf lettering is original.

ABOVE CENTER

Wooden staircase spindles have been cut down the middle lengthwise to provide a decorative detail for the shelves of a well-proportioned but plain hotel bookcase.

ABOVE RIGHT

Roof slates salvaged from a fire-damaged chapel cover a large floor area in a corner bistro.

OPPOSITE LEFT

Once installed in a small-town mansion, this floor was found piled in buckets in a reclamation yard. Although badly damaged, it was reassembled and relaid, with any missing sections cleverly matched up.

OPPOSITE CENTER

This well-worn but delicately patterned terra-cotta floor once belonged in a historic and rather grand townhouse.

OPPOSITE RIGHT

This oak staircase, designed for a converted stable block, has a curved oak stall partition forming the handrail. The iron supports and elm boards on the wall behind the staircase were reclaimed from the original building.

RIGHT

This balcony was built in a converted barn to divide a bedroom from the seating area below. The supports were made from driftwood, dried and air blasted with crushed walnut shells, and the rail and base from aged oak.

Wood for flooring is probably the most commonly reclaimed and reused material. Oak cut from turn-of-the-century farm buildings, pitch pine planks cut from a Victorian-era mill, a parquet floor in some exotic hardwood rescued from a modest downtown office building, and yellow pine from a dismantled factory all cry out to be rescued. Most striking of all the recent reclamation projects we have seen was an interlocking gymnasium floor that was taken up, its original markings preserved, and relaid in an apparently random pattern – a seemingly simple but time-consuming task. Where time and money are involved, it is easy to see why so many good-quality materials are dumped or destroyed by contractors anxious to meet their work deadlines.

It's all in the details. Details are the molten lead that filled the nail holes in a reclaimed slate floor or the simplicity of a block of wood used to prop open a door; the care the craftsman has taken to sand and shape a handrail; the choice of color in a casually placed object. All those things that accentuate, add interest, and make a room complete make an important contribution to the overall design.

Ornamental and decorative detail can be seen in the unknown origins of textured leather molding in an entrance hall; a split wooden staircase spindle that adds another dimension to an otherwise ordinary bookcase; the gold-leaf lettering on a mahogany door in an upscale townhome; and the distinctive walnut shell blasted driftwood balcony in a converted barn. All of these details have a beauty — fascinating, functionless, but exquisite in their shapes and hues.

Not all design and detail needs to be purely decorative. The original and still-functional wooden lock on a salvaged antique oak door, the plain metal rods that perfectly complement a reclaimed oak staircase rescued from the same building, and a matte black cast-iron window grill are practical features. At the same time, these details help to break up the design lines and relieve the eye – each of them pure and simple, and yet precise.

SPINDLE BOOKCASE

EQUIPMENT

Pliers
Bench saw or band saw
Tenon saw
Hammer
¾-inch wood chisel
Craft knife (optional)
Sandpaper
Electric drill
Drill bit to fit 3-inch screws
Screwdriver
Waxing brush or stiff-bristled paintbrush
Soft polishing brush
Soft cotton rags

MATERIALS

Several stair spindles
Old bookcase
1¾-inch paneling nails
Wood glue
Four wooden bun feet
Four 3-inch screws
Antique brown furniture wax

METHOD

1 Before you begin the construction of this bookcase, the spindles must be split in half along their length. It is possible, but extremely time-consuming, to do this with a handsaw. A much better result can be achieved if the spindles are cut with a bench or band saw. Before you start cutting, remember to remove any nails that are in the spindles; failure to do this may damage your tools and, more importantly, may cause the spindle to be snapped, injuring the operator.

2 Lay the bookcase on its back on a work surface, select two half-spindles for the sides of the bookcase, trim them to size with the tenon saw, and secure them temporarily in place with the paneling nails. For the shelves, we have used spindles cut so that two opposing pieces cut from the one spindle make a balanced pattern on each shelf. If you want to achieve a more idiosyncratic appearance, use one whole cut spindle for each shelf front. Shape the ends where they butt against the spindles attached to the bookcase sides with the chisel or craft knife and sandpaper to get a tight fit. Secure the spindles temporarily with paneling nails.

3 Remove all the temporarily fitted spindles, apply the wood glue to them, then replace them and secure them in place with paneling nails. If your bookcase is not fitted with feet, the spindle fitted to the bottom shelf may prevent it from standing properly. To eliminate this problem, add feet to raise the bookcase slightly off the floor. We used softwood bun feet made from cut-down old tent pole finials. Drill though each foot from the underside, apply wood glue, and secure the feet to the bottom corners of the bookcase with the 3-inch screws.

4 Put the bookcase on one side to allow the glue to dry thoroughly. When the glue is dry, apply the antique brown furniture wax with the waxing brush or stiff-bristled paintbrush, paying particular attention to brushing the wax into the corners and crevices of the spindle moldings. Rub the wax into the wood with a soft cotton rag and let it dry. Polish the wood with the soft polishing brush and finish it with a clean cotton rag. A greater density of color can be achieved with a second application of wax, and the finish can be maintained by occasional polishing with a soft cloth.

Safety note

If you are using power-cutting equipment, particularly a bench or band saw, use eye protection. Protective gloves should also be used for this project.

Spindles are the turned supports for the banister rail on a staircase. Crafted in many different lengths, they were made in the millions when wood-turning machinery was introduced, so they are easy to find. Matching or mismatched, barley twist or plain, spindles split in half make a decorative and inexpensive molding that will enhance a modest shelf unit. Split spindles can adorn all sorts of other furniture, from kitchen and bathroom cupboards to wooden mirrors. In this chapter, we even show you how to turn one into an elegant candlestick.

You could make this project leaving both the bookcase and spindles in their original painted state. However, if you want to do this, all of the painted surfaces should be cleaned, rubbed down with sandpaper, and undercoated before being repainted. Old bookcases and spindles often have several layers of paint, and the thickness of these coats can obscure some of the finer and more attractive details. To achieve the best results, we recommend that the bookcase and spindles be stripped.

Stripping can be done using a commercially available paint stripper, but this is a labor-intensive and unpleasant job that requires protective gloves and clothing. It is much easier to have your bookcase and spindles stripped by one of the many professional stripping services that use a hot caustic bath to get excellent results.

BEDSPRING CANDLE HOLDERS

EQUIPMENT

Fine-grade steel wool
Metal polish
Soft cotton rags

MATERIALS

Bedsprings
Clear lacquer spray
Globe-shaped candles

METHOD

1 Gently remove any corrosion from the bedsprings using the steel wool, taking care not to rub off the copper plating. Apply the metal polish with a soft cotton rag and burnish the springs with a clean rag. Spray the springs with the clear lacquer to preserve the finish and to prevent tarnishing. Place a globe-shaped candle in the top of each spring.

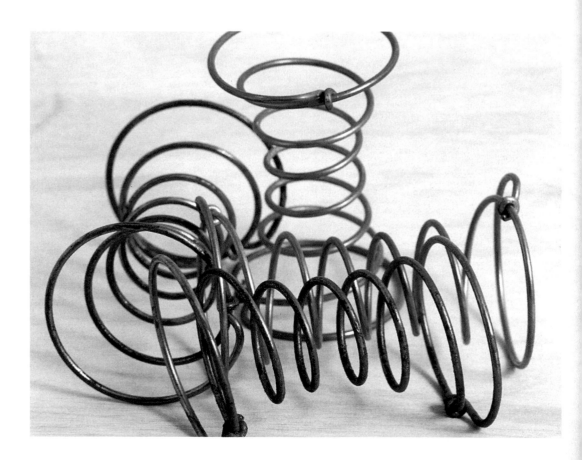

They may not be as elegant as a pair of solid silver candlesticks passed down through the family over several generations, but our bedspring candle holders are certain to become conversation pieces. They illustrate the point that even the most unlikely object can be turned into something desirable, and these coiled candle holders are both unusual and, more importantly, fun. Like many people, we have collected candlesticks in many different sizes and materials, from ceramics, glass, and metal to a set of five we designed and had turned by a local craftsman from fallen, diseased sycamore branches.

We have candles in Victorian ink bottles, tea lights in dimpled glasses found at garage sales, and others in small terra-cotta flower pots that we covered with gold and silver leaf to create a festive Christmas table display. As long as the candle fits securely into its receptacle, there is no limit to the number of objects that can be adapted to become candle holders. Flickering candlelight can illuminate every room of your home!

Scrap yards and flea markets are good hunting grounds, and at one we managed to salvage a number of these copper-plated steel bed or chair springs with the plating still intact. The coiled, almost sculptural shape of these springs with their globe-shaped candles suggests that they may have been commissioned by a master metal smith.

WOOD BLOCK TABLE

EQUIPMENT

Tape measure
Large framing square
Chalk or felt-tipped pen
Chain saw
Coarse-grit sanding disc
Angle grinder
Fine-grit sanding disc

MATERIALS

Large wooden block or post
Scrap wood

Safety note

Chain saws are extremely dangerous. If you are unfamiliar with their use, seek professional help. Always wear full protective clothing and eye protection when using a chain saw. Wear eye protection and a dust mask when sanding with an angle grinder.

METHOD

1 Measure the wooden block and calculate how it can be cut into two equal parts, both having ends that are square. Translate these measurements onto the wooden block using the framing square and the chalk or felt-tipped pen. Prop the block on the scrap wood so that it is raised off the ground and, being careful to follow the chalk or ink marks, squarely cut off one end of the block with the chain saw. Continue cutting with the chain saw until you have two equally sized blocks and until you are satisfied that the ends are square.

2 Attach the coarse-grit sanding disc to the angle grinder and remove any rough, discolored, or damaged wood from the sides and one end of the blocks; work slowly along the length of the blocks to minimize unsightly sanding marks. Finish to a smooth surface with the angle grinder and fine-grit sanding disc.

The finished blocks, complete with marks from the chain saw on their exposed tops, make extremely attractive occasional or lamp tables, perfect for a minimalist interior.

Unlikely as it may seem, these unusually large chunks of wood, which weigh enough to make you regret not doing some weight-training before you move them, once supported metal crash barriers between opposing lanes of a highway. Now that these wooden barriers are being replaced by metal dividers, we were able to acquire them at an affordable price.

Not wanting to compromise the masculine shape and powerful form of the supports, we felt that our best option was to make them more manageable by cutting them in half, making two smaller cubes. With the warmth of the honey gold wood, they are beautiful in their simplicity, works of art, set off with a ceramic pot and placed on either side of our Railway Bed (see page 40).

If you have difficulty locating a similar highway barrier, any large wooden block will serve just as well, and the project is ideally suited to an old tree trunk, squared off to size.

SPINDLE CANDLESTICK

EQUIPMENT

Hammer
Sandpaper
Tape measure
Pencil
Electric drill
1-inch spade drill bit
Pliers
Tenon saw
Steel square
1½-inch wood chisel
Craft knife
C-clamp
Soft cotton rags

MATERIALS

7-inch square of ½-inch-thick plywood or
    medium-density fiberboard
7-inch square of 1-inch-thick softwood
    plank
Wood glue
1¼-inch paneling nails
Stair spindle

This elegant candlestick was made from a turned wooden spindle. Found in differing lengths and designs in most reclamation yards, spindles are commonly made of softwood, although some can be made of hardwood.

Because so many spindles were made and there are not many uses for them, many recycling yards end up burning them for firewood. Spindles are very often varnished or painted when acquired, but they can be professionally stripped or stripped by hand with commercial paint stripper, as we did to the spindle used for this project. Time-consuming and unpleasant though it is, we were able to achieve the bleached, aged effect we sought.

Stripped spindles can be waxed and polished, or left unstripped and repainted if preferred. However, they should be rubbed down and primed before a new coat of paint is applied. We chose to leave the spindle unpolished and selected the 7-inch-square piece of 1-inch softwood plank to match its color and texture. You may choose to make any length of candlestick from old spindles, the size being dependent only on the length of the spindle used. Some spindle patterns have square moldings along their length, and these can be trimmed off to create shorter candlesticks.

SPINDLE CANDLESTICK

METHOD

1 Join the squares of plywood and softwood together with wood glue and nail them together with the 1¼-inch paneling nails. By gluing plywood or medium-density fiberboard to the softwood, you will prevent it from distorting and will ensure that the candlestick has a flat base for stability. Use the sandpaper to smooth off the sawed edges.

2 When the glue has dried, mark the center of the softwood square with the pencil, place the base on a piece of waste wood, and with the electric drill and 1-inch spade bit, drill a hole through both the softwood and the plywood underneath. For a neat finish, drill until the tip of the bit emerges, then turn over the square and complete the hole, drilling from the plywood side.

3 Take the spindle, use the pliers to remove any nails, then trim both ends square with the tenon saw. Select which end of the spindle will be the top and which is to be inserted into the base. (The end with the shorter section of square molding should form the top.) Sand off the sawed edges on the top end.

4 Draw a line with a pencil and the steel square around the bottom of the spindle 1½ inches from the end. Use the tenon saw to make a cut on each face of the spindle to leave about 1 inch of uncut wood at the center. Pry off the cut wood with the wood chisel to leave a core of approximately 1 inch at the end of the spindle. Trim the core to the exact measurement with the craft knife and sandpaper.

5 Turn the spindle around so that you are able to work on the top of it. Then clamp the spindle to the work surface with the C-clamp to hold it securely in place. Using the pencil, mark the center at the top of the end of the spindle and carefully drill a hole approximately ¾ inches deep at that point using the electric drill and the spade bit.

6 Apply the wood glue to the trimmed 1-inch end of the spindle and insert that end into the previously drilled 1-inch hole made in the wooden base. Trim off any wood that protrudes below the bottom of the base and make sure that the inserted spindle is vertical. Then use the soft cotton rag to wipe off any residual wood glue and let it dry.

HIP TILE WALL LIGHT

EQUIPMENT

Wire brush
Battery-powered electric drill
Masonry drill bit
Pencil
Electrician's screwdriver

MATERIALS

Clay roof hip tile
Scrap wood
Angled lamp holder
5 rawlplugs
Two 1½-inch screws
Electric light bulb (60 watt maximum)
Three 2½-inch screws

METHOD

1 Select a hip tile with a curve that, when placed on a flat surface, is sufficiently deep to house the angled lamp holder and electric light bulb easily. Place the tile on the work surface and remove any residual cement, lichen, or unsightly stains with the wire brush. With the concave side down, drill three holes with the electric drill and masonry bit, one at the center of the apex and one at each of the bottom corners. It is a good idea to drill through the tile into a piece of scrap wood, and drill carefully to prevent the tile from being damaged by the emerging drill bit. After the tile is drilled, put it to one side.

2 Make sure that the power is turned off at the main switch. Hold the angled lamp holder over the wires emerging from the wall in the location you want to attach the lamp. Mark the screw holes on the wall with the pencil and put the tile to one side. Use the battery-operated electric drill and masonry bit to drill holes approximately 1½ inches deep at the pencil marks and insert a rawlplug into each hole. Be careful not to drill into concealed wires. Attach the wires emerging from the wall securely to the back of the angled lamp holder, then attach the lamp holder to the wall with the 1½-inch screws driven into the rawlplugs.

3 Place the light bulb in the lamp holder and place the hip tile carefully over it in the desired position. For down-lighting, the opening should face down; for up-lighting, the opening should face up. Mark the holes drilled in the tile on the wall with the pencil and put the tile to one side. Drill holes at least 2 inches deep at the three marked points, being very careful not to drill through concealed electric wires, and insert the rawlplugs. Replace the hip tile in position and secure it to the wall using the 2½-inch screws driven into the rawlplugs.

Clay hip tiles are extremely heavy, so make sure that the finished light is securely attached to the wall and that the fittings are strong enough to take the weight. For safety, make sure that the light bulb does not touch either the wall or the rear of the tile. When you are satisfied with the appearance of your hip tile wall light, turn on the power.

Safety note

Electricity is dangerous; consult a qualified and experienced electrician before you do any electrical work. Always turn off the electricity at the main switch before starting any work. When drilling close to a wall light fixture, be very careful not to damage wires inside the wall.

Wall lights can add a quality of light and ambience to a room that is impossible to achieve with ceiling lights. The variety of wall lights that can be bought from interior design and lighting shops is extensive, but many salvaged materials can be used to make unique and attractive alternatives.

Old car headlights can be adapted to serve as wall lighting, just as other car parts, including hubcaps fitted to wire holders, can be converted into stunning shaded wall lights. The everyday metal kitchen colander cries out to be a wall light. In fact, there is no reason why you can't make a wall light out of almost anything that suits your fancy.

We have selected hip tiles for this project because they are asy to find, inexpensive to buy, and come in numerous different shapes, patterns, and sizes. We have seen a number of different hip, ridge, and roofing tiles in many innovative interiors, and examples of some of these are illustrated elsewhere in this book.

Finally, hip tiles can be used as up-lighting, with the opening at the top, or turned over, as we demonstrate in this project, as down-lighting to illuminate a painting or a piece of furniture, or to provide a muted atmosphere and unusual lighting.

The enormous elm screw, oak barrel, and aged chopping block were salvaged from a Pennsylvania cider mill. The salon mirror was found at auction, the old oak panel is soon to be part of a New York interior, while the pump handles await transformation into the legs of an occasional table. Even the floor of this storage barn is reclaimed, salvaged from the decking of a ship sunk in Lake Erie.

We are all slowly becoming more environmentally aware, religiously recycling our empty bottles and old newspapers, but in reality in considerable demand, and many reclamation dealers would jump for joy at the prospect of handling the hardwood parquet

HOW TO GET IT, HOW TO DO IT

most of us merely pay lip service to recycling and conservation.

Currently less than 5 percent of all reusable materials are recycled, and perhaps the most striking example is in the building industry. Demolition contractors know that much of what they destroy has a commercial value. Old bricks are in great demand but generally end up as fill; structural timbers, the life-blood of many reclaimed furniture makers, are often used as firewood; cast-iron radiators and ceramic bathroom fixtures are floors that are frequently ripped up and taken to dumps and landfill sites.

Demolition contractors and building developers know that the return they could get for these materials is outweighed by the time it would take to remove and find a sales outlet for them. Even the large amount of scrap metal that is available no longer fetches the price it once did and ends up discarded, further straining our already hard pressed and expensive landfill sites.

TOP LEFT

Sought-after cast-iron radiators, crates of stone, an old cider millstone, and a wood-framed fishing lodge await buyers at a Northeast recycling yard.

TOP CENTER

A pile of old triple Roman roof tiles and a number of increasingly rare glass tiles wait to be used on the roof of an addition to an old farmhouse.

TOP RIGHT

A stack of fine terra-cotta pipes and drains discovered during recent land drainage work await conversion into lamps at a salvage artist's workshop.

BOTTOM

An interesting variety of "green" oak scraps from massive roof beams that were made for a century-old New Jersey farmhouse ceiling.

Fortunately, there is a growing awareness of the problem and an increase in the small number of people trying to do something about it. The decision to use old materials should not be driven by conscience alone. Salvaged items were often made with materials and a commitment to craftsmanship that is sadly lacking in their modern counterparts, and some would argue that salvaged goods are often far more beautiful. A wrought-iron support bracket recently seen at a reclamation yard was a fine example of a Victorian craftsman adding time-consuming embellishments to a part of the structure that was revealed only when the bracket was removed from its original location.

Softwood used for utilitarian objects in the past was often sourced from species that are no longer harvested or was cut from timber of a size not found in today's commercial forests. The grain, texture, and color of many reclaimed timbers are almost impossible to find in modern wood, old handmade bricks can never be replicated, and the patina, shape, and color of stone and slate that have been worn by the feet of generations is difficult to emulate.

While it is no longer true that all reclaimed materials are less expensive than their modern alternatives, inexpensive raw materials for re-use or conversion into new and different purposes are all around us. Construction dumpsters are an obvious source of useful items, auctions are well worth attending, junk and thrift shops can offer exciting finds, and even salvaged metal merchants will sell items for their scrap value. Don't forget yard and garage sales, local consignment and antique shops, and the attics of friends and relatives.

Reclamation yards are the place to find a vast resource of architectural antiques and reclaimed and salvaged materials all under one roof. Their number has proliferated in recent years. A few years ago, enthusiasts Thornton Kay and Hazel Matravers established SALVO, the organization that today is recognized as being the hallmark of the reliable dealer. SALVO has a worldwide membership committed to the observance of its voluntary code, which is designed to promote ethical reclamation and prevent the trade in stolen artifacts or items removed from listed buildings.

SALVO publishes a regular newsletter that contains information about dealers in architectural antiques, reclaimed materials, and antique garden ornaments, as well as demolition companies, architects, craftsmen, and numerous other professionals. SALVO's Web site (www.salvo.co.uk) includes the home pages of a number of its members, along with contact information for each one.

The Internet is an expanding source of information and, increasingly, reclaimed materials. A number of state and local authorities regularly update Web information on people and organizations selling and looking for salvaged items (see page 142). There are many worthwhile sites for restoration enthusiasts, and many offer free e-mail newsletters to subscribers, which include useful information and contacts for would-be house renovators.

Travel at home and abroad stimulates inspiration for designs and new uses for reclaimed materials. It also presents a chance to rescue materials that you may be lucky enough to come across. In southern Virginia, we discovered a lot of discarded but fine handmade bricks that we later used to make a beautiful floor. A trip to Boston yielded a former garden gate that we transformed into a headboard for a bed.

A visit to Spain resulted in a return flight carrying ancient olive jars (some with the residual oil still in them) as hand luggage. We used the jars very successfully as decorative additions to our country garden. While driving through France, we found a pile of old tiles at the edge of a forest where we had stopped for a picnic.

Wherever you locate your salvaged materials, whether searching for a particular piece or discovering something "just too good to miss," use your imagination, do a bit of creative thinking when looking for alternative approaches for their use, and treat them with respect. However modest they may be, these objects have a history, and besides owning something that is unique, you will have made some small dent in the blanket of apathy that surrounds all things considered past their "useful life."

HOW TO DO IT

In *Salvage Style in Your Home,* we have shown how simple salvaged items can be transformed into things of beauty. Not everything we have used for these projects will be available to you, but almost all the projects we have demonstrated can be adapted to use things you find or that you may already own.

Most reclamation dealers are glad to give you the benefit of their knowledge – indeed, it's sometimes hard to pull yourself away from an enthusiast! Never be afraid to ask questions because if the dealer doesn't know the answer, then he or she generally know someone who does.

Here we outline a number of the more common techniques used in the restoration or salvage trade. Some you can do yourself, others will need to be done professionally.

LEFT

Faucets and water pipes have been welded to a brass samovar, giving this bathroom in a Boston restaurant a feel of the exotic East.

BELOW

Three different reclaimed doors: The one on the left is one of a pair of outer softwood louver doors with fretted insert, original hinges, catches, and paintwork, which was preserved with several applications of tung oil. The inner door on the right is glazed with an oak frame, and behind it is a pair of double doors with their original stained glass, used to hide kitchen paraphernalia.

AGING METALS

You may have to give new metals an aged look. Virtually all metals tarnish over time, old iron door hardware rusts, brass tarnishes, and zinc finishes dull, and when new materials are used in salvage projects, their brashness can spoil the appearance. While there are a number of commercially available "cosmetic" treatments that can be bought in hobby and craft shops, often a simple process can accelerate natural aging, and the end result is more authentic.

ZINC

We use large quantities of perforated zinc to create new food pantries from old cupboards. New perforated zinc, which is available from most hardware stores or building suppliers, is bright and shiny and doesn't resemble the fragile zinc used on old pieces of furniture. We simply dissolve copper sulfate crystals in a little water and wipe the solution over the new zinc with a soft cloth or sponge. You will see the difference immediately. Copper sulfate crystals, also known as blue vitriol, are available at craft stores or by special order at pharmacies.

BRASS

Door hardware designs have changed little over the years, and new brass fixtures are invaluable when you cannot find their antique counterparts.

For years, we have kept a container of old and rather smelly malt vinegar in our workshop – with an airtight lid! New brass fittings are dropped into the vinegar, left overnight, and placed in the open air for another 24 hours. In that time, the surface of the brass will start to discolor and dull. If this does not happen, the piece may have been covered with paint. Strip the paint with paint remover or caustic soda, wash, and repeat the dipping process.

STEEL

Water is the age-old enemy of iron and steel. Vast sums of money are spent on preventing rust in industry and business. However, we frequently have to encourage steel to rust in order to match it to older pieces. We simply leave the steel outdoors, and the weather does our work for us. Rusting can be encouraged by heating the metal and then dousing it in water before leaving it outside for oxidation to take place. We find this process particularly useful for removing paint from and for aging iron chain and black japanned steel fittings.

CLEANING AND POLISHING

Some materials need to be aged, but in other circumstances the same material must be cleaned or polished. The conditions in which some salvaged materials are found can discourage all but the most enthusiastic craftsmen. Wood once used for cattle stalls can be encrusted with manure, beams of hardwood timber may be saturated with fungi, and roll-top baths likely will be chipped, stained, and rusted. However, all of these objects can be rescued and restored to something approaching their former glory.

WOOD

Most hard and softwood salvaged lumber is found heavily soiled or stained. Surface soiling can be removed with a pressure washer, but remember the wood must be dry before it is re-used. It is important to dry wood under cover and stack it so that air can circulate around and in between the pieces.

Severely damaged or dirty lumber can be shot or grit blasted, which will remove the surface layer of softer material and the grain as well as the dirt – a little dramatic but quite effective. A labor-intensive alternative is cleaning the wood with a wire brush or a revolving wire or grit wheel.

All salvaged wood should be treated for rot, insect infestation, and fungal attack before re-use, or the problem might spread to other lumber in your stock. Cuprinol, the company that helped us with this book, produces a range of effective wood treatment products as well as numerous color finishes for interior wood. (See the section Useful Contacts on page 140.)

It is difficult to give a polished finish to rough-cut or sawed timber, but planed or smooth-surfaced lumber will benefit from any of the color treatments or waxes that are available today. Choose the color you use carefully because you want to use the finish to enhance rather than mask the wood's natural grain.

SLATE

We have used and discussed slate at length in various projects in this book. Slate is found in a wide range of subtle colors and is now imported into the United States from India, Mexico, China, and Africa, as well as many other countries. Slate is used on roofs, floors, walls, and household work surfaces.

There are numerous commercial slate polishes and sealants that any building materials supplier will be happy to sell to you. But it may be worth considering the traditional Welsh custom of applying sour milk to slate floors to achieve a subtle finish. We have tried it, and it works. The fat present in the milk is absorbed by the slate, while the drying liquid gives the surface a soft shine. Although the application process is little smelly, the result is effective and can be easily removed with hot water and detergent.

One technique for dealing with the nail holes that mar many reclaimed slates is to fill the holes with molten lead after the slates are laid. We have found the best method of application is to use a blowtorch and lead soldering wire. Unwanted drips and splashes are easily removed, and the end result is well worth the effort. One note of caution: Always be careful to hold a blowtorch upright, wear protective glasses, gloves, and clothing, and never apply a blowtorch to a wet slate, or an explosion may result.

BRASS

Compare modern and antique brass and you will note a subtle difference in color. Modern brass has more copper in its composition, and professional restorers always keep a stock of old brass on hand to use when restoring antique pieces. Elbow grease and metal polish are the prerequisites for polishing brass – or call in the professionals. Metal antique restorers swear that some brands of cola soft drinks are as effective at cleaning brass as most commercial polishes, although we have seen them use buffing machines and industrial compounds to clean and polish the keys, door hardware, old musical instruments, and chandeliers.

Some abrasive polishing can be done with electric hand tools, and buffing brushes and compounds can be obtained from industrial finishing and jewelry suppliers.

STEEL AND IRON

Elbow grease, wire brushes and metal polish are the standard tools for polishing steel, although a buffing machine makes short work of this labor-intensive job. Numerous attachments are made for electric hand tools that are particularly useful for cleaning and polishing weathered and pitted iron. Black and Decker, one of the companies that helped us in the production of this book, produces a useful range of electric hand tools and attachments. See the section Useful Contacts on page 140 for details.

Cleaned and polished iron and steel can be protected with a coating of transparent furniture wax, but it is more effective to spray them with a commercial metal paint.

To get a blackened appearance, wrought and cast iron can be given an authentic (and protective) finish with stove blacking paste. This is a messy job but results in a finish far more attractive than paint can ever achieve.

BRICK AND TERRA-COTTA

Old and stained bricks and terra-cotta can be cleaned with muriatic acid, which is sold at building supply companies. This is a job where gloves, protective glasses and clothing, and a face mask are essential. Seek professional advice before attempting such cleaning, or better still, leave it to the professionals.

Many sealants and polishes formulated especially for terra-cotta floors are commercially available. Most are adequate for the job, and the best course of action is to seek a recommendation from your supplier or a previous user.

We have experimented very successfully with cutting bricks in half and using them as flooring. Old handmade bricks, when cut, can reveal a fascinating swirl of colors and patterns formed when the clay used to make them was hand cast into wooden molds before firing. These patterns can be accentuated and the surface protected with an application of raw linseed oil — another messy but ultimately worthwhile job.

TOP

When this northern California house was renovated, a butler's pantry was created using reclaimed materials, such as the ceramic sink, faucets, and drainboard.

BOTTOM

In this striking bedroom, the bed was constructed from wooden balcony supports cut in half to create a simple but effective look, blending well with the reclaimed floor.

REMOVING CHROME

Many brass faucets and bathroom fixtures started their life plated with chrome. Chrome plating can be removed by electrolysis in sulfuric acid, but a simpler process is by dipping the fixtures into hydrochloric acid, although this can result in the brass pitting. Neither process should be attempted by anyone other than a professional, who has the proper equipment and experience.

PRESERVING WOOD

Most cases of wood rot and worm and fungal attack can be treated with commercial products. All require that you wear protective clothing, and always read and follow the manufacturer's instructions. All salvaged lumber should be treated before use.

Treated wood that has softened can be repaired with a commercial wood hardener, and holes can be filled with wood filler. Cuprinol manufactures an effective hardener and a range of wood fillers. See the section Useful Contacts on page 140 for details.

STRIPPING WOOD

If you want to remove paint from old wood, there are several ways to do this. However, you must be aware that old wood may have been painted with a lead-based product. This dangerous material is highly toxic, and you must take every precaution to prevent inhalation of lead-based paint dust. Always wear a dust mask when sanding, especially with power tools.

The most obvious method of paint removal is sanding, either with sanding tools or by

hand. Sanding is time-consuming, and not only is it difficult to remove paint from intricate areas, but it also may remove some of the wood surface as well.

Heat stripping was once the most common method of paint stripping available to the home decorator. Paraffin heat guns have been replaced by gas and electrical guns, but these tend to scorch the wood in all but the most experienced hands.

Chemical stripping is extremely effective and is particularly useful for stripping glued, fragile, or intricate objects. It is unpleasant, messy, and you must wear protective eyewear and clothing. However, it has less effect on the color of the wood than caustic stripping.

Caustic stripping is done by professional strippers, which immerse the wood in a hot caustic-filled tank. This process is effective on oil-based paints but not on water-based paints. The process can color the dipped wood, especially if the caustic bath has been in use for some time. It can also loosen glued joints and fixtures. It is not advisable to strip hardwoods in hot or cold caustic baths.

USEFUL CONTACTS

TOOLS & SUPPLIES

BLACK AND DECKER
Tel: 800-544-6986
Web site:
www.blackanddecker.com
Electrical and battery-powered hand tools for the professional and hobbyist.

HOME DEPOT
Tel: 800-430-3376
Web site:
www.homedepot.com
Screws, nails, hardware, tools, plumbing and electrical supplies, lumber.

LOWES
Tel: 336-658-7100
Web site: www.lowes.com
Screws, nails, hardware, tools, plumbing and electrical supplies, lumber.

WOOD TREATMENT PRODUCTS

CUPRINOL PRODUCTS
101 Prospect Avenue
Cleveland, OH 44115
Tel: 800-424-5837
Web site: www.cuprinol.com
Wood treatment products, stains, and color washes for internal and external use. A useful advice line for customer queries.

INFORMATION ON RECLAMATION & ARCHITECTURAL ANTIQUES DEALERS & SERVICES

SALVO
18 Ford Village
Berwick-upon-Tweed
Northumberland TD15 2QG
United Kingdom
Tel: 01890 820333
Fax: 1890 820499
E-mail: tk@salvoweb.com
Web site: www.salvoweb.com
Publishers of information on architectural antiques, reclamation dealers, and reclaimed building materials. Originators of the SALVO Code

and the Salvo Code Dealer list. The SALVO Web site links many different reclamation dealers from all over the world.

RECLAMATION AND ARCHITECTURAL ANTIQUES DEALERS

ADKINS ARCHITECTURAL ANTIQUES
3515 Fannin Street
Houston, TX 77004
Tel: 713-522-6547
Fax: 713-529-8253
Architectural antiques, mantels, stained glass windows, lighting and plumbing fixtures, doors and door hardware, garden decor, patio furniture, urns, benches, fountains.

ADMAC SALVAGE
111 Saranac Street
Littleton, NH 03561
Tel: 603-444-1200
Web site:
www.musar.com/Admac
Architectural antiques and collectibles, barn boards, tools, banisters, mantels, windows, doors, cabinets, plumbing and lighting fixtures, office furniture, electrical supplies.

AMERICAN SALVAGE
7001 NW 27th Avenue
Miami, FL 33147
Tel: 305-691-7001
Fax: 305-691-0001
Architectural salvage and hotel, restaurant, and building supplies.

AMERICAN TIMBERS LLC
P.O. Box 430
Canterbury, CT 06331
Tel: 800-461-8660
Fax: 860-546-9334
Recycled lumber.

ANTIQUE ARTICLES
P.O. Box 72
North Billerica, MA 01862
Tel/Fax: 978-663-8083
Web site:
www.antiquearticles.com
Antique tiles, complete fireplace surrounds.

ARCHITECTURAL ACCENTS
2711 Piedmont Road
Atlanta, GA 30305
Tel: 404-266-8700
Fax: 404-266-0074
Over 30,000 square feet of architectural antiques.

ARCHITECTURAL ANTIQUE AND SALVAGE CO. OF SANTA BARBARA
726 Anacapa Street
Santa Barbara, CA 93101
Tel: 805-905-2446
Iron gates, grates, rails, garden objects, doors, designer furniture.

ARCHITECTURAL ANTIQUES EXCHANGE
715 N. Second Street
Philadelphia, PA 19123
Tel: 215-922-3669
Fax: 215-922-3680
E-mail: AAExchange@aol.com
Web site: www.
architecturalantiques.com
Architectural salvage, bars, wood and marble mantels, leaded and beveled glass, urns, mirrors, signs, paneling, street lamps, stained glass, doors, ironwork, carved furniture.

ARCHITECTURAL ARTIFACTS
2207 Carimer Street
Denver, CO 80033
Tel: 303-292-6812
Fax: 303-403-0886
Exterior and interior period doors, tin ceilings, porch columns, hardware, pedestal sinks, claw-foot bathtubs, lighting and plumbing fixtures.

ARCHITECTURAL ARTIFACTS
20 South Ontario
Toledo, OH 43602
Tel: 419-243-6916
Fax: 419-243-0094
Architectural antiques, statuary, iron, plumbing, urns, benches, columns, stained glass, doors, hardware, lighting, mantels, religious items, stairway parts.

ARCHITECTURAL ELEMENTS
818 East 8th Street
Sioux Falls, SD 57103
Tel/fax: 605-339-9646
Architectural antiques, salvaged millwork, doors, moldings, flooring.

ARCHITECTURAL EMPORIUM
207 Adams Avenue
Canonsburg, PA 15317
Tel: 724-746-4301
Web site: www.
architectural-emporium.com
Architectural antiques, doors, chandeliers, light fixtures, wall sconces, mantels, hardware, stained glass, windows, terra-cotta tiles, cupboards.

ARCHITECTURAL SALVAGE
1215 Delaware Street
Denver, CO 80204
Tel: 303-615-5432
Architectural antiques.

ARCHITECTURAL SALVAGE
618 East Broadway
Louisville, KY 40202
Tel: 502-589-0670
Fax: 502-589-4024
Mantels, light fixtures, doors, hardware, leaded glass windows, ironwork.

ARCHITECTURAL SALVAGE
103 West Michigan Avenue
Grass Lake, MI 49240
Tel: 517-522-8715
Antique building materials, beveled and stained glass, mantels, doors, hardware, lighting.

ARCHITECTURAL SALVAGE INC.
3 Mill Street
Exeter, NH 03833
Tel/fax: 603-773-5635
Web site:
www.oldhousesalvage.com
Doorways, molding, hardware, lighting and bath fixtures, doors, mantels, windows, flooring, stair parts, floor registers, ironwork.

ARCHITECTURAL SALVAGE WAREHOUSE
53 Main Street
Burlington, VT 05401
Tel: 802-658-5011
E-mail: salvage@together.net
Web site: www.
architecturalsalvagevt.com
Architectural antiques, mantels, doors, windows, hardware, plumbing, lighting, columns.

ARTIFACTS AND ANTIQUES
105 Heady Drive
Nashville, TN 37205
Tel: 615-354-1267
Fax: 615-354-0617
E-mail:
artifacts@mindspring.com
Architectural antiques, garden ornaments, lighting.

THE BARNWOOD CONNECTION
91 Bull Road
Barto, PA 19504
Tel: 610-845-3101
Fax: 610-845-3167
Used lumber.

BELCHER'S
2505 West Hillview Drive
Dalton, GA 30721
Tel: 706-259-3482
Pre-Civil War log cabins, weathered barn siding, split rails, hand-hewn beams, handmade doors.

BIG SPRING PRESERVATION GROUP
The Atrium Suites
111 North Central Avenue
Suite 5
Knoxville, TN 37902
Tel: 423-637-2585
Fax: 423-637-1589
Salvaged early log houses, log barns, outbuildings, post-and-beam frame barns, timber-frame houses, salvaged flooring, barn boards, doors, windows, mantels.

CARAVATI'S INC.
104 East 2nd Street
Richmond, VA 23224
Tel: 804-232-4175
Fax: 804-233-7109
E-mail: webmaster@
recentruins.com
Web site:
www.recentruins.com
Architectural salvage, stained-
glass windows, bathtubs,
ornamental iron, shutters,
windows, moldings.

**CAROLINA ARCHITECTURAL
SALVAGE AND COGAN'S
ANTIQUES**
110 South Palmer Street
Ridgeway, SC 29130
Tel: 803-337-3939
E-mail: jcogan@usit.net
Web site:
www.usit.com/ccogan
Architectural antiques, lighting
fixtures, mantels, stained-
glass windows, doors, newel
posts and columns, bathroom
sinks, bathtubs, iron fencing,
gates, window guards,
shutters, store fixtures,
bookcases, furniture.

**CHESTNUT WOODWORKING
& ANTIQUE FLOORING CO.**
P.O. Box 204
West Cornwall, CT 06796
Tel: 860-672-4300
Fax: 860-672-2441
Antique flooring in chestnut
oak, pine, and hemlock.

CHRISTOPHER HESS INC.
3931 Cedar Drive
Walnutport, PA 18088
Tel: 610-760-9533
E-mail:
chbarndawg@earthlink.net
Web site: www.
christopherhessinc.com
Antique wood flooring and
lumber.

COLONIAL ANTIQUES
5000 West 96th Street
Indianapolis, IN 46268
Tel: 317-873-2727
Architectural salvage, lighting,
mantels, hardware, garden
items, stained glass, doors.

THE EMPORIUM
1800 Westheimer Road
Houston, TX 77098
Tel: 800-528-3808
or 713-528-3808
Fax: 713-528-5494
E-mail:
Emporium@NeoSoft.com
Web site: www.the-
emporium.com
Architectural antiques, lighting,
doors, gates, fountains,
hinges, plumbing fixtures,
stained glass, mantels,
Victorian gingerbread trim,
newel posts, handrails,
pressed tin ceilings, moldings,
patio/garden urns, statuary
and birdbaths, mirrors, cast
metal patio furniture.

**THE ENGLISH ANTIQUES
WAREHOUSE**
North Carolina Highway 105
Banner Elk, NC 28604
Tel: 828-963-4274
or 888-POT-TOPS
Web site: www.
englishantiqueimports.com
Architectural antiques, antique
English chimneypots,
farmhouse furniture, wrought-
iron garden seats.

**FLORIDA VICTORIAN
ARCHITECTURAL
ANTIQUES**
112 West Georgia Avenue
DeLand, FL 32720
Tel: 904-734-9300
Fax: 904-734-1150
E-mail:
info@floridavictorian.com
Web site:
www.floridavictorian.com
Antique building materials,
doors, windows, flooring,
hardware, claw-foot bathtubs,
mantels, doorknobs.

**GOVERNOR'S ANTIQUES &
ARCHITECTURAL
MATERIALS**
8000 Antique Lane
Mechanicsville, VA 23116
Tel: 804-746-1030
Fax: 804-730-8308
Architectural antiques, iron fence
gates, carved stone, statues,
garden and yard furniture,
doors, slate, mantels, Civil War
relics, marble.

HARBOR BAZAAR
5590 Main
Lexington, MI 48450
Tel: 810-359-5333
Web site:
www.tias.com/stores/bazaar
Furniture, glass, lamps, lighting.

**HORSEFEATHERS
ARCHITECTURAL
ANTIQUES**
346 Connecticut Street
Buffalo, NY 14213
Tel: 716-882-1581
Fax: 716-882-0215
Architectural salvage and
antiques, furniture, doors,
mantels, lighting, stained
glass, Victorian gingerbread,
urns, statuary, fencing,
columns.

**KIMBERLY'S OLD-HOUSE
GALLERY**
1600 Jonquill Lane
Wausau, WI 54401
Tel: 715-359-5077
Architectural antiques, building
salvage.

MIDWEST SALVAGE
628 13th Avenue
Sidney, NE 69162
Tel: 308-254-4387
Framing and siding lumber
salvaged from barns.

THE MOBILE MERCHANT
1052 Virginia Avenue
Indianapolis, IN 46203
Tel: 317-264-9968
E-mail: mobile@
antiqueresources.com
Web site: www.
antiqueresources.com/mobile
Architectural antiques, fences,
stained glass, mantels,
lighting, bars, doors, windows.

**ODOM REUSABLE BUILDING
MATERIALS**
926 S. Airport Road
Traverse City, MI 49686
Tel: 231-946-4883
E-mail:
reusebruce@coslink.net
Web site: www.
odomusedbuildingmaterials.
com
Used construction materials.

OLDE GOOD THINGS
124 W. 24th Street
New York, NY 10011
Tel: 212-989-8401
or 888-551-7333
E-mail: feedbk@
oldegoodthings.com
Web site: oldegoodthings.com
Architectural antiques, hardware,
doorknobs, mantels, doors,
iron, lighting, bronze, brass,
columns, stones, mirrors,
stained glass.

OLD HOUSE PARTS CO. INC.
24 Blue Wave Mall
Kennebunk, ME 04043
Tel: 207-985-1999
Fax: 207-985-1911
E-mail: restoration@
oldhouseparts.com
Web site:
www.oldhouseparts.com
Architectural salvage, antiques,
construction material, molding,
windows, hardware, mantels,
trim, furnishings, stairways,
barn boards, sashes, doors.

PINCH OF THE PAST INC.
109 W. Broughton Street
Savannah, GA 31401
Tel/fax: 912-232-5563
Architectural antiques, furniture,
lighting, mantels, columns,
doors, hardware, ironwork,
plaster ornaments.

PRESERVATION HALL
23 Rankin Avenue
Asheville, NC 28801
Tel: 828-251-2823
Web site: www.
preservation-hall.com
Architectural antiques, doors,
windows, plumbing fixtures,
mantels, flooring, millwork, iron.

RECYCLING THE PAST
381 North Main Street, Route 9
Barnegat, NJ 08005
Tel: 609-660-9790
Web site: www.
recyclingthepast.com
Architectural antiques, iron gates
and fencing, hardware, tile,
kitchen and bath fixtures,
vintage building materials,
doors, windows, stained glass,
mantels.

SALVAGE DEPOT INC.
6516 N.W. Grand Avenue
Glendale, AZ 85301
Tel: 602-931-4115
Fax: 602-931-4118
Architectural salvage.

SALVAGE HEAVEN
6633 West National Avenue
West Allis, WI 53214
Tel: 414-329-7170
Fax: 414-329-7172
Fixtures, architectural elements,
furniture.

SALVAGE ONE
1524 South Sangamon Street
Chicago, IL 60608
Tel: 312-733-0098
Fax: 312-733-6829
American and European
architectural and building
elements, millwork, plumbing
and lighting fixtures, garden
ornaments, art glass.

UNITED HOUSE WRECKING
535 Hope Street
Stamford, CT 06906
Tel: 203-348-5371
Fax: 203-961-9472
Antiques, furniture, stained glass,
wall decorations, bakers' racks,
entry doors, windows, mantels,
fireplace accessories, plumbing
and lighting fixtures, fencing,
outdoor furniture, fountains,
statuary, cupolas,
weathervanes.

**VERMONT SALVAGE
EXCHANGE**
Gates Street
P.O. Box 453
White River Junction, VT 05001
Tel: 802-295-7616
Fax: 802-295-5744
Web site: www.
vermontsalvage.com
Architectural salvage, reclaimed
doors, staircases, windows,
mantels, stone, columns,
lighting and bathroom fixtures,
cabinetry, hardware.

WATER STREET ANTIQUES
P.O. Box 1707
Sutter Creek, CA 95685
Tel: 209-223-4189
Fax: 209-223-2534
Antique wood.

REGIONAL RECYCLING ORGANIZATIONS

APPALACHIAN REGIONAL RECYCLING CONSORTIUM
6580 Valley Center Drive
Box 21
Radford, VA 24141
Tel: 540-639-9314
Web site: www.civic.bev.net/
pdc/arrc/trader.html

ARIZONA RECYCLING COALITION
101 E. Central
Phoenix, AZ 85004
Tel: 602-256-3170
Web site: www.azrc.org

ARKANSAS RECYCLING COALITION
P.O. Box 25734
Little Rock, AR 72221
Tel: 510-227-6979

ASSOCIATED RECYCLERS OF MONTANA
458 Charles
Billings, MT 59101
Tel: 406-252-5721

ASSOCIATED RECYCLERS OF WISCONSIN
P.O. Box 44008
Madison, WI 53744
Tel: 608-277-1978

ASSOCIATION OF IDAHO RECYCLERS
P.O. Box 3746
Boise, ID 83703
Tel: 208-321-2761

ASSOCIATION OF NEW JERSEY RECYCLERS
120 Finderne Avenue
Bridgewater, NJ 08807
Tel: 908-722-7575
Web site: www.anjr.com

ASSOCIATION OF OHIO RECYCLERS
P.O. Box 70
Mt. Vernon, OH 43050
Tel: 614-397-7641

ASSOCIATION OF OREGON RECYCLERS
P.O. Box 483
Gresham, OR 97030
Tel: 503-661-4475

ASSOCIATION OF VERMONT RECYCLERS
P.O. Box 1244
Montpelier, VT 05601
Tel: 802-229-1833
Web site: www.vtrecyclers.org

CALIFORNIA RESOURCE RECOVERY ASSOCIATION
4395 Gold Trail Way
Loomis, CA 95650
Tel: 916-652-4450
Web site: www.crra.com

CAROLINA RECYCLING ASSOCIATION
7330 Chapel Hill Road #207
Raleigh, NC
Tel: 919-851-8444
Web site: www.
cra-recycle.org

COLORADO RECYCLES
8745 W. 14th Avenue #216
Lakewood, CO 80215
Tel: 303-231-9972
Web site: www.
colorado-recycles.org

CONNECTICUT RECYCLERS COALITION
P.O. Box 4038
Old Lyme, CT 06371
Tel: 203-774-1253

GEORGIA RECYCLING COALITION
2508 Kiner Court
Lawrenceville, GA 30243
Tel: 770-822-9308
Web site: www.
georgiarecycles.org

ILLINOIS RECYCLING ASSOCIATION
P.O. Box 3717
Oak Park, IL 60303
Tel: 708-358-0050
Web site: www.
ilrecyclingassn.org

INDIANA RECYCLING COALITION
P.O. Box 20444
Indianapolis, IN 46220
Tel: 317-283-6226
Web site: www.papertrail.com

IOWA RECYCLING ASSOCIATION
2742 S.E. Market Street
Des Moines, IA 50317
Tel: 515-265-4275
Web site: www.recycleiowa.org

KANSAS BUSINESS & INDUSTRY RECYCLING PROGRAM
2933 S.W. Woodside Drive
Suite C
Topeka, KS 66614
Tel: 785-273-2405

KENTUCKY RECYCLING ASSOCIATION
P.O. Box 19904
Louisville, KY 40259
Tel: 606-257-5671

MAINE RESOURCE RECOVERY ASSOCIATION
P.O. Box 1838
Bangor, ME 04402
Tel: 207-942-6772

MARYLAND RECYCLERS COALITION
584 Bellerive Drive, Suite 3-D
Annapolis, MD 21401
Tel: 410-974-4472
Web site:
www.marylandrecyclers.org

MASS RECYCLE
25 West Street
Boston, MA 02111
Tel: 617-338-0244

MICHIGAN RECYCLING COALITION
P.O. Box 10240
Lansing, MI 48901
Tel: 517-371-7073
Web site: www.mienv.org/mrc

MINNESOTA WASTE ASSOCIATION
1030 Evergreen Trail
Lino Lake, MN 55014
Tel: 651-785-8807

MISSOURI STATE RECYCLING ASSOCIATION
435 Westport Road
Kansas City, MO 64111
Tel: 417-466-2758

NEBRASKA STATE RECYCLING ASSOCIATION
1941 South 42nd Street #512
Omaha, NE 68105
Tel: 402-444-4188

NEVADA RECYCLING COALITION
P.O. Box 70393
Reno, NV 89507
Tel: 775-333-9322

NEW YORK ASSOCIATION OF REDUCTION, REUSE, AND RECYCLING INC.
P.O. Box 3913
Albany, NY 12203
Tel: 888-925-7329
Web site: www.nysar3.org

NORTHEAST RECYCLING COUNCIL
139 Main Street #401
Brattleboro, VT 05308
Tel: 802-254-3636
Web site: www.nerc.org

NORTHEAST RESOURCE RECOVERY ASSOCIATION
P.O. Box 721
Concord, NH 03302
Tel: 603-224-6996
Web site: www.efne.org

OKLAHOMA RECYCLING ASSOCIATION
201 West 5th, Suite 600
Tulsa, OK 74103
Tel: 918-584-0584

PENNSYLVANIA RESOURCES COUNCIL
3606 Providence Road
Newtown Square, PA 19703
Tel: 610-353-1555
Web site: www.prc.org

RECYCLEFLORIDA TODAY
1015 Highway 301 S., #2425
Tampa, FL 33619
Tel: 813-441-6425
Web site: www.enviroworld.
com/resources/RFT.html

RECYCLING ASSOCIATION OF MINNESOTA
890 Dawn Avenue
Shoreview, MN 55126
Tel: 651-486-0455
Web site: www.
ram-recycle.netoffc.com

RECYCLING COALITION OF TEXAS
P.O. Box 2359
Austin, TX 78768
Tel: 512-469-6079
Web site: www.recycletx.org

RECYCLING COALITION OF UTAH
P.O. Box 112045
Salt Lake City, UT 84147
Tel: 435-755-9469
Web site: www.
recycle.utah.org/RCU.html

SOUTH CAROLINA RECYCLING ASSOCIATION
1205 Pendleton Street #517
Columbia, SC 29201
Tel: 803-734-0143

SOUTH DAKOTA RECYCLING COALITION
P.O. Box 90358
Sioux Falls, SD 57105
Tel: 605-333-2341

TENNESSEE RECYCLING COALITION
P.O. Box 23796
Nashville, TN 37202
Tel: 615-230-3035

WASHINGTON REFUSE & RECYCLING ASSOCIATION
711 South Capitol Way
P.O. Box 1486
Olympia, WA 98507
Tel: 360-943-8859
Web site: www.wrra.org

WYOMING RECYCLING ASSOCIATION
P.O. Box 539
Laramie, WY 82070
Tel: 307-332-6924
Web site: www.1wyo.com

INDEX

ACKNOWLEDGMENTS

This full-length mirror demonstrates an imaginative use of weathered timber from a disused farm gate. Note the clever use of the original gate hinges and the bolts at the bottom of the mirror that conceal balancing weights behind.

Our thanks to Kyle Cathie Publishers, editors **Kate Oldfield** and **Helen Woodhall**, our photographer **Tim Winter,** and his assistant **Jo Fairclough.**

Our thanks also to the following companies who generously helped us with equipment, materials, and advice:

Black and Decker
Hand and power tools for the professional and handyman
Cuprinol Ltd
Timber treatment products and decorative color stains and finishes
Screwfix Direct
Hardware and tools by overnight mail-order

Also thanks to those who kindly allowed us to photograph their homes and businesses:

Angela Coombes and
Michael Hewitt

Peter and **Sarah Fineman**

Peter Watson and
Jacqui Spencer

Elizabeth and **Crispin Deacon**
Saltmoor House, Saltmoor
Burrowbridge, Somerset
TA7 0RL

Arne Ringner, proprietor
Byzantium Restaurant
2 Portwall Lane, Bristol
BS1 6NB
E-mail: info@byzantium.co.uk
Web site: www.byzantium.co.uk

Roger and **Monty Saul**
Charlton House Hotel
Shepton Mallet, Somerset
BA4 4PR
E-mail: reservations-charltonhouse@btinternet.com
Web site: www.
mulberry-england.co.uk

Thanks to Bob Whitfield for his shots of the interior of the home of Hank and Sophia Terry.

And thanks to the following artists and craftspeople:

Candace Bahouth, mosaic artist

Pete Chapman and
Jeff Blagdon, Au Temps Perdu

Haydn Davies, Wells Reclamation

John Edmonds, John Edmonds Cabinet Makers

Lawrence Harper, Harper's Bazaar

Steve Horler, Frome Reclamation

Thornton Kay and
Hazel Matravers, SALVO

Robert Mills, Robert Mills Reclamation

Tim and **Nicky Ovel**, Country Brocante

Henry and **Mary Porter**, Porter Design

Hank and **Sophia Terry,** Milo Design

John and **Mike Tyler**, JAT Reclamation

Richard Wallace and
Corrinna Sargood, furniture maker and artist

Mark Watson of Watson Bertram and Fell, architects